"Vern Poythress explores the pathways of human reasoning with simplicity and clarity. What is especially intriguing and unusual about this book, however, is the way in which he grounds human reasoning in the triune God, strongly emphasizing its analogical dimension. As a result, he helps us to think carefully about careful thinking, and to do so in the presence of our Lord. There is much of value in this book that will stimulate your thinking—and your reasoning!"

Joel R. Beeke, President, Puritan Reformed Theological Seminary

"We live in an age in which people have largely forgotten how to think. They emote, they assert, and they yell; but one of the most powerful human goods— our rational capacity—has atrophied for lack of use. Our superintelligent, suprarational God has given us intellectual gifts to navigate the world, and it's high time we recover how we are to use them. In this much-needed volume, Vern Poythress helps us to be rational without being rationalists and reasonable without forfeiting our affections. As a mathematician, theologian, and New Testament scholar, there is no one better equipped to help us redeem reason than Poythress."

C. Ben Mitchell, professor; author, *Ethics and Moral Reasoning: A Student's Guide*

Crossway Books by Vern S. Poythress

Chance and the Sovereignty of God

In the Beginning Was the Word

Inerrancy and the Gospels

Inerrancy and Worldview

Interpreting Eden

Logic

The Lordship of Christ

The Miracles of Jesus

Reading the Word of God in the Presence of God

Redeeming Mathematics

Redeeming Our Thinking about History

Redeeming Philosophy

Redeeming Reason

Redeeming Science

Redeeming Sociology

Theophany

Truth, Theology, and Perspective

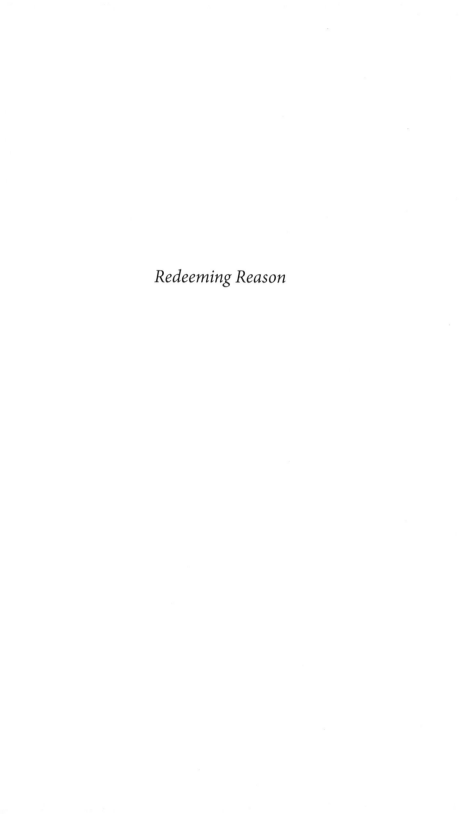

Redeeming Reason

Redeeming Reason

A God-Centered Approach

Vern S. Poythress

WHEATON, ILLINOIS

Trade paperback ISBN: 978-1-4335-8731-3
ePub ISBN: 978-1-4335-8734-4
PDF ISBN: 978-1-4335-8732-0
Mobipocket ISBN: 978-1-4335-8733-7

Library of Congress Cataloging-in-Publication Data

Names: Poythress, Vern S., author.
Title: Redeeming reason : a God-centered approach / Vern S. Poythress.
Description: Wheaton, Illinois : Crossway, 2023. | Includes bibliographical references and index.
Identifiers: LCCN 2022019534 (print) | LCCN 2022019535 (ebook) | ISBN 9781433587313 (trade paperback) | ISBN 9781433587320 (pdf) | ISBN 9781433587337 (mobipocket) | ISBN 9781433587344 (epub)
Subjects: LCSH: Faith and reason—Christianity.
Classification: LCC BT50 .P69 2023 (print) | LCC BT50 (ebook) | DDC 231/.042—dc23/eng/20221123
LC record available at https://lccn.loc.gov/2022019534
LC ebook record available at https://lccn.loc.gov/2022019535

Crossway is a publishing ministry of Good News Publishers.

BP		31	30	29	28	27	26	25	24	23
15	14	13	12	11	10	9	8	7	6	5	4	3	2	1

To my wife, Diane

Contents

Tables

Diagrams

Introduction

HOW DO WE GROW in reasoning well? One way is to study logic. There are already books that explore this route, with a focus on formal logic.[1] Here, we want to go beyond that study to explore the nature of human *reasoning*, which is a broader subject.[2] Reasoning includes formal logic as a subdivision. It also includes informal reasoning, such as occurs in jury deliberations, general decision-making, and evaluation of causal explanations. How well are we doing in the use of reasoning?

Our goal is to explore how human reasoning depends on God. God is the source of all truth and all rationality. Our communion with God makes a difference in how we think and reason. We also want to take into account how human reasoning is corrupted by sin and how it can be renewed by the redemption that Christ accomplished.

One main area to explore is the use of analogy in reasoning. Our human reasoning is analogous to God's original rationality, but it is derivative. Our understanding of truth is likewise derivative. We will consider how the use of analogy is pervasive in reasoning, and how analogy depends on guidance from a larger context. God himself is the ultimate context. Renewal in our knowledge of God therefore affects all of our reasoning.

---

1 Vern S. Poythress, *Logic: A God-Centered Approach to the Foundation of Western Thought* (Wheaton, IL: Crossway, 2013).

2 Stephen Toulmin's book *The Uses of Argument* (Cambridge: Cambridge University Press, 1958), is one example that uses the term "logic" more broadly to describe many forms of reasoning; "idealised logic" is one label he uses to designate what others might call "formal logic" or simply "logic." What label we use is a secondary issue.

1

Where to Start in Redeeming Reason

SO WHERE CAN WE START, if we want to improve in our reasoning?

Reason, Intuition, and Emotion

People who take pride in reasoning sometimes complain about others who are swayed by emotion or impulse or intuition. For example, let us say that Bob buys the latest cool gadget on impulse. Then he finds that he does not really need it. Not only that, but if he had first looked up some consumer evaluations, he would have found a better and less expensive alternative. He regrets his impulse buying. His impulses have overcome his better rational judgment.

But people may also regret decisions they have made on the basis of rational arguments. Let us say that Sue's conscience warns her not to cheat on her income tax. Conscience is an intuitive source for decisions. But instead of listening to her conscience, she makes excuses. She produces a whole series of arguments for why the government does not deserve her loyalty, why her way of cheating on her taxes will never be found out, or why hers is an exceptional case. She is reasoning things out. Perhaps she is quite careful. She had *better* be careful, if she thinks she can create a scheme that will not be found out. But the whole project exemplifies a situation where reasoning is being used *against* the truth and *against* genuine moral principles rather than in support of the truth and against mere impulse.

John Frame, in his book *The Doctrine of the Knowledge of God*,[1] points out that human knowledge involves several aspects. Certainly reason has a role. But so does our emotional life, and so do human impressions from our situation. In none of these realms is human knowledge infallible. We are fallen, sinful human beings. And sin infects all of life. All three aspects—reasoning, emotions, and our impressions of the situation—need reform. All three need redemption, we might say.

In the Bible, redemption comes from God the Father, through Christ, who is the one true Redeemer (John 14:6; Acts 4:12; 1 Tim. 2:5). Strictly speaking, God redeems *people*, not ideas. But the people who are redeemed have their minds and their hearts renewed (Rom. 12:2): "Do not be conformed to this world, but be transformed by the renewal of your mind, that by testing you may discern what is the will of God, what is good and acceptable and perfect." So, secondarily, we can talk about the redemption of a person's mind.[2] This renewal includes a renewal of how we reason, as well as a renewal of our emotional life and our intuitions. What does a renewal of reasoning look like? We will see that it involves communion with God himself, and that it involves the proper use of *analogy*, as a key aspect of reasoning.

Mystery and Transparency

Let us begin by reflecting on formal logic, as a subdivision of human reasoning. It is an impressive subdivision. Can we be instructed by logic in a way that renews all human reasoning?

Aristotle's syllogisms and modern forms of symbolic logic may seem on the surface to offer us clear, cogent, transparent ways of reasoning. Moreover, much insight into rationality can be gained by using these modes of reasoning as models or perspectives on human rationality in general. But there are difficulties underneath

---

1   John M. Frame, *The Doctrine of the Knowledge of God* (Phillipsburg, NJ: P&R, 1987).

2   Vern S. Poythress, *The Lordship of Christ: Serving Our Savior All of the Time, in All of Life, with All of Our Heart* (Wheaton, IL: Crossway, 2016), 96–99.

the surface.[3] The appearance of transparency is achieved by crafting special environments that enable the core patterns in formal logic to possess their impressive cleanness.

In the end, the difficulty traces back to the very nature of human reasoning. Our reasoning powers reach limits when we undertake

---

3   Vern S. Poythress, *Logic: A God-Centered Approach to the Foundation of Western Thought* (Wheaton, IL: Crossway, 2013), esp. part I.C; Vern S. Poythress, "Semiotic Analysis of Symbolic Logic Using Tagmemic Theory: With Implications for Analytic Philosophy," *Semiotica* 2021, https://doi.org/10.1515/sem-2020-0018, https://frame-poythress.org /a-semiotic-analysis-of-symbolic-logic-using-tagmemic-theory-with-implications-for -analytic-philosophy/; Stephen Toulmin, *The Uses of Argument* (Cambridge: Cambridge University Press, 1958).

Toulmin's concerns in *Uses of Argument* overlap with those in this book. He does not want the pattern of analytic reasoning in the syllogism to become the exclusive standard for all reasoning whatsoever (esp. in his ch. 4). But an additional difficulty that he does not directly address is the question of where we get the norms for considering some reasoning—perhaps syllogistic reasoning—as superior to other forms, and whether therefore other forms of reasoning are "deficient" or in need of correction. There are at least two positions, namely that many forms of practical reasoning are deficient, or that they are okay as they stand.

Philosophers drawn to the ideal of perfect mastery and perfect transparency in reasoning are tempted to make syllogisms a central example, because syllogisms seem to approach the ideal that those philosophers desire. Ordinary forms of reasoning appear to be deficient, when measured against this ideal. But in many of the contexts of philosophical discussion, this ideal of perfect transparency is corrupted by a lack of distinction between divine knowledge and human knowledge (Poythress, *Logic*, ch. 7 and part I.C). God's knowledge is the standard for human knowledge. But God's knowledge is also distinct from human knowledge. God's knowledge is never transparent to us who are human. There is always mystery. So the goal of perfect transparency is muddled. The ideal of transparency is suspect, for religious reasons. It is also suspect for practical reasons. It is never actually achieved!

On the other hand, consider the other position, namely, that many cases of practical reasoning are okay as they stand. If there is no deep reliance on a divine standard, who is to say that normal, practical uses of reasoning are all right? Toulmin rightly sees gaps between ordinary forms of reasoning and a philosophical ideal. But how does he or any of us know that the ordinary forms are actually okay, according to the proper norm? The fact that human beings in various fields *treat* the reasoning in that field as acceptable may be a merely sociological observation. Maybe the reasoning is nevertheless deficient or defective, and this deficiency is disconcertingly widespread. So some philosophers search for a route to "save" us from our alleged follies. The ordinary person on the street does not think his reasoning needs saving. The Christian, on the other hand, acknowledges the need for salvation from God, as well as the need for God to sustain and ground our reasoning powers themselves.

to reason about God. God is not man (Num. 23:19). God's thoughts are not our thoughts (Isa. 55:9). Nevertheless, there is a relation between God and man. According to the Bible, man is made in the image of God (Gen. 1:26–27). As one aspect of being in the image of God, we have abilities to appreciate truth. We can know truth. In fact, we can know God: "For although they *knew God*, they did not honor him as God or give thanks to him, . . ." (Rom. 1:21). The verse in Romans indicates that some kind of knowledge of God extends even to unbelievers.

But we do not know God in the way and to the extent that God knows himself. There is mystery. If there is mystery in our knowledge of God, there will also be mystery at a deep level in our knowledge of everything else. All our knowledge imitates God's original knowledge. And this imitation is mysterious, because God's knowledge is mysterious.

We find mysteries at every point in our understanding of God.[4] Does that leave no room for human reasoning? No, there is room. But our human reasoning at its best merely reflects God's own rational self-consistency, which is the original standard. If there is room for our reasoning, what is the shape of that reasoning? In what ways should our thinking be transformed by the renewing of our minds (Rom. 12:2)?

Renewal in Romans 12:1–2

What does Romans 12:1–2 actually say about the renewal of our minds? Here are the verses:

> I appeal to you therefore, brothers, by the mercies of God, to present your bodies as a living sacrifice, holy and acceptable to God, which is your spiritual worship. Do not be conformed to this world, but *be transformed by the renewal of your mind*, that by testing you may discern what is the will of God, what is good and acceptable and perfect.

---

4 Vern S. Poythress, *The Mystery of the Trinity: A Trinitarian Approach to the Attributes of God* (Phillipsburg, NJ: P&R, 2020), esp. ch. 2.

The verses do not become specific about just what is involved in this transformation and renewal. Other verses indicate that when we belong to Christ, we are to be progressively conformed to his image:

> And we all, with unveiled face, beholding the glory of the Lord, *are being transformed* into the same image from one degree of glory to another. (2 Cor. 3:18)

> Rather, speaking the truth in love, we are to *grow up in every way into him* who is the head, into Christ, . . . (Eph. 4:15)

This conformity includes the mind as well as other aspects of our nature:

> "For who has understood the mind of the Lord so as to instruct him?" But we have the mind of Christ. (1 Cor. 2:16)

The context of Romans 12:1–2 indicates that our renewal means discerning "the will of God, what is good and acceptable and perfect." The next verse, verse 3, specifically exhorts us to humility in what we think about ourselves: "not to think of himself more highly than he ought to think, but to think with sober judgment, each according to the measure of faith that God has assigned." What now does it mean to know God's will, and what might be our limitations in knowing it? The description of God's will as "good and acceptable and perfect" calls to mind the positive descriptions of the word of God, as a guide to God's will.

> The law of the LORD is perfect,
>   reviving the soul;
> the testimony of the LORD is sure,
>   making wise the simple;
> the precepts of the LORD are right,
>   rejoicing the heart;
> the commandment of the LORD is pure,

enlightening the eyes;
the fear of the Lord is clean,
    enduring forever;
the rules of the Lord are true,
    and righteous altogether.
More to be desired are they than gold,
    even much fine gold;
sweeter also than honey
    and drippings of the honeycomb. (Ps. 19:7–10)

In addition to these words in Psalm 19, Psalm 119 is a long poem celebrating the goodness and perfection of God's word:

Your testimonies are my delight;
    they are my counselors. (v. 24)

As "counselors," God's testimonies show what his will is. The law of the Lord is "perfect" (Ps. 19:7; 119:96). The righteous man "meditates [on it] day and night" (Ps. 1:2).

At the heart of renewal of our minds is the knowledge of God in Christ (Matt. 11:27; John 17:3), which includes having "the mind of Christ" (1 Cor. 2:16). The Bible does not focus on a renewal of some technical aspect of reasoning, but on a comprehensive and deep renewal that we cannot fully explain or make self-conscious. If there are changes in some more technical way, they are subordinate to a more fundamental renewal. Renewal is not primarily renewal through *self* reflection, but renewal through a saving relation to God. In that saving relation, God's word in the Bible has a central role. We are to meditate on it. The absorption of the word can be compared to "eating" it:

Yours words were found, and I *ate them*,
    and your words became to me a joy
    and the delight of my heart. (Jer. 15:16)

In a similar way, Jesus tells us to abide in him, and that his words should abide in us (John 15:1–7).

Within this pattern of comprehensive renewal, we may nevertheless ask whether we can learn to think and reason better, in accord with the Bible's content.

Reasoning Forward to New Conceptions of Reasoning

The difficulties in dealing with reasoning include a kind of circularity. How do we use reasoning to *reform* reasoning? How can we arrive at a refined concept of human reasoning if we are not already there, that is, if we are not already reasoning correctly? And if we are *not* going to use reasoning, are we going to proceed forward by an irrational leap? If it is a leap not already controlled by reason, how can it give us assurance that the place at which we arrive is reasonable?

Ludwig Wittgenstein in his remarkable work *Tractatus Logico-Philosophicus* sketched out what he thought was one way to do this.[5] He built an account of the world that was like a conceptual ladder. When one reached the top of the ladder, one had a correct view of the world. And, from the standpoint of that view, one understood that the ladder itself was not correct. One threw it away.

We are *not* going to use a route like that. It is difficult to see how one could have full confidence in the endpoint if one saw that the route itself depended on illusion.

But what is the alternative? The alternative is to reason forward soundly the whole way up the ladder. But to do so, we must already, at the beginning, have the correct view of reason. If we are not already there, it seems that we cannot get there.

This difficulty seems great because the questions about correct reason have typically arisen in a larger environment, produced ultimately by the fall of man and the desire for human autonomy. Adam and Eve desired to "be like God, knowing good and evil" (Gen. 3:5). They

---

5   Ludwig Wittgenstein, *Tractatus Logico-Philosophicus: The German Text of Logisch-philosophische Abhandlung* (London: Routledge & Kegan Paul/New York: Humanities Press, 1963). The book is remarkable, but very far from a Christian approach.

wanted a kind of independence that was rebellious at its core. Ever since, philosophers have often set out to reason independently. They think they must depend on themselves and their reason, not on God.

Reasoning from Revelation

The difficulty does not have the same shape when we adopt a Christian point of view. God breaks into the neat circles of our autonomy. Or we might say that he breaks into the circular trap of being unable to conceive of an alternative. The alternative form of reasoning is an alternative rooted in God. And then, secondarily, it is an alternative that comes to us through God revealing truth to us. He reveals himself, and also reveals truths about himself, about ourselves, and about the world.

This alternative makes sense only if God first rescues us out of our sinful, fallen, rebellious condition. He sends the Holy Spirit to open our eyes and to renew our hearts. God gives us new birth (John 3:3–5). Then we are willing to admit that we are creatures and that we are dependent. We admit that we need the Holy Spirit to give us spiritual understanding (1 Cor. 2:14–16).

God reveals truths in general revelation (through the world around us) and in special revelation (the Bible). God reveals himself in nature, and in the very mind of man. Studying God using only the input from nature is sometimes called "natural theology." (We must distinguish "natural theology" from "a theology of nature," such as we might learn from the Bible itself and what it says about nature.) In this book we are not going to do natural theology, independent of Scripture. It is treacherous for us, who have minds corrupted by sin, to detach ourselves from the instruction in Scripture when we observe nature. So the Bible, as infallible verbal revelation from God, is our source of true knowledge in our present discussion.

Though the Bible is true, our understanding of the Bible is not flawless. So neither is our exposition of the nature of reasoning going to be flawless. But because God exists and speaks to us in the Bible, our exposition can still make progress in comparison with the conceptions of the godless world.

Reasoning in a Context

Our reasoning takes place in the context of the rest of our lives. And that context includes many things that we take to be true. That is true of me as well. It is not feasible within the scope of one book to defend everything with a full exposition. So readers will have to bear with the fact that this book sometimes refers to other sources.

We are going to be reasoning things out. It may appear, then, that sometimes we are reasoning purely in the abstract. But that is not the case. Rather, we want to be thoroughly influenced by the Bible's teaching. We are reasoning in a way that intends to trace out some of the natural harmony in different aspects of the Bible's teaching. But it would take much more space to confirm *in detail* that the Bible supports what is said here.

PART I

GOD AS THE SOURCE
OF RATIONALITY

*We consider how God is rational and is the source for
rationality in human beings and in the world.*

2

God's Rationality

IF WE ARE TO HAVE a foundation for human reasoning, that foundation must be found ultimately in God. God is absolute. He is not dependent on the world or on anything in the world. Neither is he dependent on us. We are dependent on him—thoroughly. That includes our reasoning. Human reasoning does have meaning. That meaning derives ultimately from God, who created us in his image (Gen. 1:26–27) and sustains us day by day.

Dependence on God

How might we confirm that our reasoning is dependent on God? There are many ways. One may argue that the laws of logic reveal God and display the attributes of God.[1] A similar type of argument can be used starting with scientific laws or simply with truth.[2] Let us consider a similar argument here, starting with principles for reasoning.

One principle for reasoning is the law of noncontradiction.[3] Two contradictory statements cannot both be true. It is a valid principle. It holds true everywhere in the universe. It holds true at all times. It is

---

1 Vern S. Poythress, *Logic: A God-Centered Approach to the Foundation of Western Thought* (Wheaton, IL: Crossway, 2013), ch. 7.

2 Vern S. Poythress, *Redeeming Science: A God-Centered Approach* (Wheaton, IL: Crossway, 2006), chs. 1 and 14.

3 Many sources list the law of noncontradiction as one of three fundamental laws of logic. See, for example, *Encyclopedia Britannica*, "Laws of thought: Logic," https://www .britannica.com/topic/laws-of-thought (accessed April 2, 2020).

unchangeably true. So it displays three attributes that are classically associated with God: omnipresence (being everywhere), eternality (transcending all times), and immutability (unchangeability). (See table 2.1.)

Table 2.1: Some Attributes of God and Logical Principle

Attributes of God	Attributes of Logical Principle
omnipresence	everywhere present
eternality	present at all times
immutability	does not change

The Attributes of God

We can extend the list of attributes. The principle of noncontradiction is not a material thing like an apple or an eraser. It is *immaterial*. It holds true with respect to statements that we might make about apples or erasers. It *applies* to material things. But it is not a "thing," an object in the world. Next, it is invisible—though visible in its implications with respect to apples or erasers. It is truthful; it is reliable.

It is omnipotent. By that we mean that nothing escapes its grip, its control. It transcends all particular cases. It is also immanent, in the sense that it operates with and in each particular case. Immateriality, invisibility, truthfulness, reliability, omnipotence, transcendence, and immanence are all attributes of God. (See table 2.2.)

Table 2.2: More Attributes of God and Logical Principle

Attributes of God	Attributes of Logical Principle
immaterial	immaterial
invisible	invisible
truthful	truthful
reliable	reliable
omnipotent	omnipotent
transcendent	transcendent
immanent	immanent

What we are seeing here is analogous to what is said in Romans 1:19–20:

> For what can be known about God is plain to them, because God has shown it to them. For his *invisible attributes*, namely, his eternal power and divine nature, have been clearly perceived, ever since the creation of the world, in the things that have been made. So they are without excuse.

Romans 1:19–20 is focusing on created things ("the things that have been made"). These created things reveal the attributes of God. In contrast to this focus on *things*, we are now focusing on *principles* governing created things. These principles also reveal the attributes of God.

A crucial question that remains is whether these eternal, immutable, and omnipotent principles are impersonal or personal. Is there one God? And is he personal?

First, is there only one God? There cannot be two omnipotents, because they would compete for control. The unified principles governing the world display unity in their source. So yes, there is only one God. This conclusion is a further confirmation of what we know from Scripture. Scripture affirms that there is only one true God (Deut. 6:4; Mark 12:29; 1 Cor. 8:6; James 2:19).

Is God personal? The Bible teaches that he is personal. Is that truth reinforced by general revelation? One route to show that God is personal is to observe that a law presupposes a lawgiver. And a lawgiver is personal. Or, if this movement seems too simple, we may observe that the governing laws or principles for the world are rational and language-like. Rationality is characteristic of persons but not of rocks. The governing laws are also language-like. We do not literally hear a voice speaking them, but we are able to express the laws in language. The complexity and articulability of the laws are characteristic of persons. (Some smart animals, such as dogs, can interpret simple verbal commands. But their understanding still falls far below our ability to use the complexities of language.)

The law of noncontradiction testifies to God. It does so because God is the source of the law and it is an expression or reflection of his character.

It presupposes God, who is the lawgiver. God is absolute, as implied in his omnipotence. He is also personal, as implied by the rational, language-like character of the principle of noncontradiction. As we observed above, it is best to understand this conclusion as an instance where we start with the Bible's revelation of God, and then see how its truths are also expressed as we look at how he rules the world. One aspect of God's rule is that he specifies and maintains the law of noncontradiction (see fig. 2.1).

Figure 2.1: God as the Source of Laws

God Is Trinity

God is the trinitarian God of the Bible. This truth is derivable from the Bible. And reading the Bible is the best route to the truth about God, because of the corruption of the human mind by sin. Quite a few books show how the doctrine of the Trinity derives from the Bible.[4] Can we see expressions of the truth of the Trinity by looking at how God displays himself in the world? And would the truth of the Trinity *also* be reflected in the nature of human reasoning?

Once we know that God is trinitarian, there are various ways in which we find expressions and reflections of his being trinitarian. We can look at God's ability to speak, or his attribute of love, or how he is the source of morality and scientific laws.[5] Instead of using one of these routes, let us focus on the norms for reasoning. We *ought to*

---

4   There is a short exposition in Vern S. Poythress, *Knowing and the Trinity: How Perspectives in Human Knowledge Imitate the Trinity* (Phillipsburg, NJ: P&R, 2018), ch. 6. For more thorough discussion one may consult Robert Letham, *The Holy Trinity: In Scripture, History, Theology, and Worship*, rev. and expanded (Phillipsburg, NJ: P&R, 2019); John Owen, *A Brief Declaration and Vindication of the Doctrine of the Trinity*, 1669, in *The Works of John Owen*, ed. William H. Goold, 16 vols. (repr., Edinburgh/Carlisle, PA: The Banner of Truth Trust, 1965), 2:365–454; John Owen, *Communion with the Triune God*, ed. Kelly M. Kapic and Justin Taylor (Wheaton, IL: Crossway, 2007).

5   Poythress, *Knowing and the Trinity*, ch. 37.

reason well. That sense of "ought" is a norm. The norms include not violating the law of noncontradiction. A source of norms has to be there, as a presupposition for the operation of laws of reasoning. The ultimate norm is God. God is absolute, since he is the ultimate norm. He is also personal, since we have to be responsible to persons, *not* to impersonal states of affairs.

The topic of norms belongs to the realm of ethics. We can set forth a more specific argument, indicating the trinitarian basis of ethics. First, let us understand that the entire realm of ethics can be viewed from each of three perspectives. (1) The *normative* perspective focuses on ethical norms (like the Ten Commandments). (2) The *situational* perspective focuses on the situations in which people must act. (3) The *existential* perspective focuses on the people in the situation, and their motivations.[6] The existential perspective is also called the *personal* perspective, because it focuses on the persons who are acting ethically. Each of these is a perspective *on the whole field* of ethics. The norms tell us that we have to apply the norms to the situation and to ourselves. So the normative perspective implicitly includes attention to the situation and to the persons who have to act morally. It therefore includes the situational perspective, which focuses on the situation, and the existential perspective, which focuses on the persons and their motives.

We may also consider what happens when we start with the situational perspective. The situation includes God, whom we should try to please and who is the source of the norms. So the situational perspective implies the normative perspective. The situation also includes ourselves and our motives. So we have to pay attention to our motives, which involves the existential perspective.

Next, consider what happens when we start with the existential perspective. We focus on our motives. And our motive should be love,

---

6   John M. Frame, "A Primer on Perspectivalism (Revised 2008)," https://frame-poythress .org/a-primer-on-perspectivalism-revised-2008/, accessed April 25, 2020; John M. Frame, *Perspectives on the Word of God: An Introduction to Christian Ethics* (Eugene, OR: Wipf & Stock, 1999).

which implies that we will pay attention to God and to what benefits our neighbor, given the situation.

So now, these three perspectives on ethics reflect the persons of the Trinity in a certain way, as follows:

> There are three perspectives [on ethics]. The authoritative character of ethics, associated with the normative perspective, derives from the authoritative character of God as the speaker of ethical rules. Ethics is pertinent to the world, which is the focus of the situational perspective. The pertinence of ethics to situations derives from the fact that contents of God's ethical speech refer to the world and situations in the world. Thus, the situational perspective, focusing on situations, derives from the content of God's speaking, which derives from the eternal Word. The existential perspective focuses on the persons who are obligated by ethics and by ethical rules. The hold that ethical rules have on persons derives from the impact of God's speech on them, which derives from the Holy Spirit as breath and recipient of God's speech. So each of the three perspectives on ethics derives from a person in God.[7]

In sum, the Father's authority is reflected in the normative character of ethics. The Son as the Word of God is reflected in the situation, which conforms to God's word. The Holy Spirit is reflected in the responsibility of persons who stand in the presence of God and receive the breath of God in the person of the Holy Spirit. (See table 2.3.)

Table 2.3: Ethics from Persons of the Trinity[8]

Persons of the Trinity	Speech Providing Ethics	Perspectives on Ethics
the Father	speaker with authority	normative perspective
the Son	speech referring to the world	situational perspective
the Holy Spirit	speech impacting and gripping people	existential perspective

---

7   Poythress, *Knowing and the Trinity*, 326.
8   Poythress, *Knowing and the Trinity*, 326, table 37.1.

We should also note that it is easy to oversimplify the relations. The Father, the Son, and the Holy Spirit indwell each other. They are all present with authority, with impact on each situation, and with impact on each person. So the correlations between a specific person and a specific function in ethics are cases where the person is preeminent. His role stands out. But he does not function in isolation from the other two persons.

We can re-express the same system of correlations, the correlations in table 2.3, using a diagram instead of a table (see fig. 2.2).

Figure 2.2: From Persons of the Trinity to Ethics

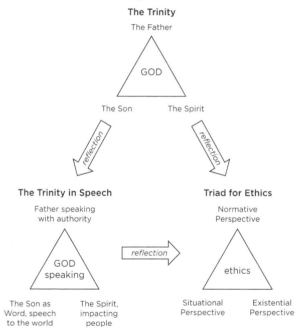

We may apply this same reasoning to the law of noncontradiction, as one norm. (1) The law of noncontradiction has to have authority; (2) it has to hold true in particular cases in the world; and (3) it has to constrain people who are thinking. These three aspects hold together, but they are also distinct. They are one form of reflection of the trinitarian character of God. In fact, in all human reasoning, and not simply with the law of noncontradiction, God is there in three respects. (1) He is there as authority; (2) he is there as *ruler* over the *world* to which reasoning applies; and (3) he is there in personal *presence* for the people who are reasoning. There are three aspects, namely authority, control (rule over the world), and presence. These three have a close relation to the three perspectives on ethics.[9] Authority is closely related to the normative perspective; control is closely related to the situational perspective (because control is control over the situation); presence is closely related to the existential perspective (it is personal presence to us who are persons with our inward motives). God is authoritative, controlling, and present. God does these three things as Father, Son, and Holy Spirit.[10]

In sum, the distinction among the three persons, the distinction of the Father, the Son, and the Holy Spirit, is reflected in the three perspectives on ethics; and this threefold distinction in turn is expressed in three aspects of God's lordship in relation to the world—the aspects of authority, control, and presence. We may summarize in a table (table 2.4).

Table 2.4: From the Trinity to Ethics to Aspects of Lordship

Persons of the Trinity	Perspectives on Ethics	Aspects of Lordship
the Father	normative perspective	authority
the Son	situational perspective	control
the Holy Spirit	existential perspective	presence

Or we may use a diagram (fig. 2.3).

9   The triad of authority, control, and presence comes from Frame, "Primer on Perspectivalism."
10   Poythress, *Knowing and the Trinity*, ch. 14.

Figure 2.3: From the Trinity to Lordly Rule and Ethics

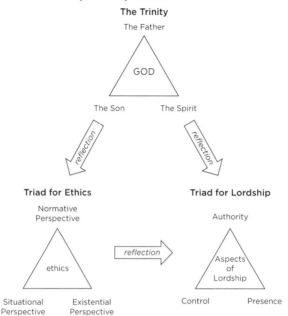

The Trinity in Speech

We may also observe that God has the capability of speech. This capability is the foundation for the language-like character of the laws of logic. God speaks eternally as the trinitarian God. The second person of the Trinity is the Word (John 1:1). The Holy Spirit is like the breath of God (Ezek. 37:10, 14), and is also one who hears what God speaks (John 16:13).[11] (See fig. 2.4.)

God speaks to the world, specifying the things in the world and how the world progresses (Gen. 1:3; Ps. 33:6, 9). God speaks in specifying the laws of human reasoning. God's speech is trinitarian, and so the laws of logic display the impress of the trinitarian character of God. All these observations are confirmations of the truth that God is the source and foundation for human reasoning.

---

11 Poythress, *Knowing and the Trinity*, chs. 8 and 37.

Figure 2.4: God Speaking Eternally in the Trinity

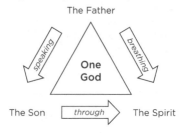

Mankind as the Image of God

God provides the environment for the operations of human reasoning in other ways. The most obvious way, perhaps, is that he created us:

> Then God said, "Let us make man *in our image, after our likeness.* And let them have dominion over the fish of the sea and over the birds of the heavens and over the livestock and over all the earth and over every creeping thing that creeps on the earth."

> So God created man *in his own image,*
>   *in the image of God* he created him;
>   male and female he created them. (Gen. 1:26–27)

Both in Genesis 1:26–27 and in Genesis 5:3, the Bible uses two terms, *image* and *likeness.* They overlap in meaning. Man is made *like* God.[12] But the more elaborate language, "in the image of God," indicates that man is like God in a number of ways, not just at one point. There is a kind of overall structural likeness, such as we might see if we compared a portrait of a person with the person himself. The Bible thus invites us to go throughout its pages and observe many ways in which mankind is like God. One way is in the use of language. God speaks in Genesis 1:3 and throughout Genesis 1. God names the light and the darkness (v. 5). God speaks to man (2:16–17). Man is clearly capable of processing language. And Adam undertakes to name the animals (2:19–20), in parallel with the instances of God's naming in Genesis 1. (See fig. 2.5.)

---

12 Poythress, *Knowing and the Trinity,* chs. 8 and 37.

Figure 2.5: God's Speech and Man's

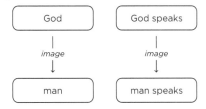

Thinking is closely related to language. If human beings can speak, it indicates that they are thinking and are also expressing what they are thinking. God also has thoughts, though they are superior to human thoughts:

> For my thoughts are not your thoughts,
>> neither are your ways my ways, declares the LORD.
> For as the heavens are higher than the earth,
>> so are my ways higher than your ways
>> and my thoughts than your thoughts. (Isa. 55:8–9)

Likewise, we may infer that God's rationality is the foundation for our rationality. Our rationality is imitative of his. But it is not on the same level, as Isaiah 55:8–9 indicates (see fig. 2.6).

Figure 2.6: God's Rationality and Man's

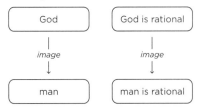

It is worth noting that we are imitators of God in more than rationality. God's rationality is one aspect of who he is. But he is also a speaking God; he is a holy God; he is a loving God; he is an all-powerful God. Rationality is not more ultimate than these other characteristics of

God. Rather, they are all ultimate. They all describe who God is. And since God is absolute, his character is not determined by something in back of him, some more ultimate principle such as rationality or love. Rather, God is loving, and God is rational, and those realities are ultimate.[13] They are the source behind all human reflections. We reflect God when we act as those who are made in the image of God.

This theme of image and reflections is significant. We want to use it as our main entrance into thinking about the nature of human reasoning.

13   Vern S. Poythress, *The Mystery of the Trinity: A Trinitarian Approach to the Attributes of God* (Phillipsburg, NJ: P&R, 2020), ch. 9.

3

God's Rationality Expressed

WE HAVE SAID that God is rational. We should say also that God is incomprehensible. As human beings, we can know God and we *do* know God (Rom. 1:19–20; John 17:3). But we do not know him completely. Nor then do we know his rationality completely. His rationality is nevertheless the starting point for our rationality, because we are made in his image.[1]

Trinitarian Rationality

God is rational. So God the Father is rational. The Son is rational. And the Holy Spirit is rational. Yet there are not three rationalities but one.[2]

This one rationality is differentiated in accordance with the mystery of the differentiation of the distinct persons of the Trinity.[3] To understand this differentiation better, we may use three principal biblical analogies for the Trinity. The three analogies are the analogy with communication, the analogy with a family, and the analogy with reflections.[4] (See fig. 3.1.)

---

1   See the discussion of the knowledge of God in Vern S. Poythress, *The Mystery of the Trinity: A Trinitarian Approach to the Attributes of God* (Phillipsburg, NJ: P&R, 2020), ch. 2.
2   We here imitate the Athanasian Creed: "So likewise the Father is almighty, the Son almighty, and the Holy Spirit almighty. And yet they are not three almighties, but one almighty."
3   See Poythress, *Mystery of the Trinity*, chs. 44–47.
4   Vern S. Poythress, *Knowing and the Trinity: How Perspectives in Human Knowledge Imitate the Trinity* (Phillipsburg, NJ: P&R, 2018), ch. 8.

Figure 3.1: Analogies for the Trinity Used in the Bible

Let us consider these one at a time.

The Analogy with Communication

The analogy with communication occurs in the Bible when the second person of the Trinity is called "the Word" (John 1:1; Rev. 19:13). Here, the implication is that God the Father is the speaker; God the Son, who is called "the Word" (John 1:14), is the speech. The Holy Spirit is not directly mentioned in these passages, but elsewhere he is compared to the breath of God (Ezek. 37:9, 10, 14) and is described as hearing the Father and the Son (John 16:13). God's speaking in the Word is eternal (John 1:1). Human speech imitates this original divine speech.

In John 1:1, the underlying Greek word is *logos*, which is related to our English word *logic*.[5] Does John 1:1 deal with logic? John 1:1–4 is closely connected to Genesis 1, where God *speaks* in order to create light, plants, the sun, and the animals. Speaking, rather than reasoning, is the more prominent focus. So in John 1:1 "the Word" rather than "logic" or "reason" is the right translation.

But still, the association with logic and with rationality is there in the background. The Greek word *logos* does have associations with reason and rational discourse. And the translation "the Word" indicates that the Word expresses God's character. His character includes his self-consistency. And when we look at Genesis 1, we see the marvelous

---

5   Vern S. Poythress, *Logic: A God-Centered Approach to the Foundation of Western Thought* (Wheaton, IL: Crossway, 2013), 69–70.

wisdom of God being expressed in his speeches. Proverbs 8 explicitly indicates that his wisdom was there when he created the world: "When he established the heavens, I [wisdom] was there" (Prov. 8:27; see also 8:28–31; Ps. 136:5). God's plan for the created world as a whole displays his wisdom. It therefore displays his rationality. God is consistent with himself. His consistency implies his rationality. Human rationality reflects that original rationality of God.

God has planned everything from before the foundation of the world (Eph. 1:4; 1 Pet. 1:20). Then he speaks in order to bring it to pass. The rationality of his plan comes to expression in the rationality of his speech. The original pattern is found in God the Father speaking the Word. We may call this original pattern the *archetype*. The rationality of the Father comes to eternal expression in the rationality of the Word. And then, when God creates the world, the rationality of the Father and the Son comes to expression in particular speeches that impress God's rational plan on the world itself—light, the expanse, the plants, the heavenly lights, and so on. The particular speeches are imitative derivatives of the archetype, which is God speaking the Word eternally. We may call these imitative derivatives *ectypes*. All this takes place in the presence of the Holy Spirit, who shows his presence when he hovers over the face of the waters in Genesis 1:2.

God is present in his word. He is present when he speaks the words that cause light to come into existence: "Let there be light" (Gen. 1:3). The words are not disconnected from him, but display his presence. God is present. And so we may also say that the Father is present; the Son is present; and the Holy Spirit is present. The relation between the archetypal speech of God, in eternity, and his speech to create the world is a relation between archetype and ectype. (See fig. 3.2.)

The analogy with human speech already suggests a close relation between speaker and speech. Among human beings, the speech represents and expresses the character of the speaker. By analogy, the Word expresses the character of God the Father. The Word is in harmony with the Father, and this harmony is a form of rationality. The rationality in the way the world works is a reflection of the original rationality of God himself.

Figure 3.2: God Speaking, Expressing Rationality

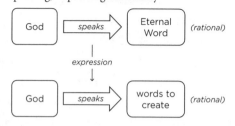

The Analogy with a Family

Next, let us consider the analogy with a family. The analogy with a family is the analogy that comes to expression when the Bible uses the names *Father* and *Son* to designate the first and second persons of the Trinity. The relation between the first and second persons of the Trinity is analogous to the relation between a human father and son. Does the Holy Spirit come into this analogy? The Holy Spirit is closely associated with the bond of love between the Father and the Son:

> For he [the Son] whom God has sent utters the words of God, for he gives the Spirit without measure. The Father *loves* the Son and has given all things into his hand. (John 3:34–35)

Figure 3.3: The Son Reflecting the Rationality of the Father

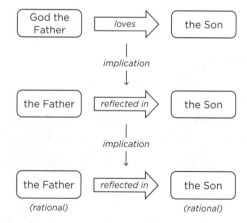

By analogy with a human family, the Father loves the Son. Or rather, at a fundamental level the analogy goes the other way. The Father and the Son in the Trinity are the archetype or original Father and Son. Earthly fathers and sons reflect the pattern of the Trinity. One way they reflect the pattern is when an earthly father loves his son. An earthly son is like his father (Gen. 5:3). By analogy, the heavenly Son is like his Father and represents him (Col. 1:15; John 14:9). Among other things, the rationality of the Father is reflected in the Son. (See fig. 3.3.)

The Analogy with Reflections

Next, let us consider the analogy with reflections. The analogy with reflections occurs in the biblical passages that say that the Son is the *image* of the Father:

> He [the Son] is the *image* of the invisible God, . . . (Col. 1:15)

> He [the Son] is the radiance of the glory of God and the *exact imprint* of his nature, . . . (Heb. 1:3)

These verses have implications similar to the terms *Father* and *Son*. The Son reflects the character of the Father, including his rationality.

Mankind as Image

The texts that speak of the Son as the image of God are later in the history of revelation than Genesis 1. But they reveal an eternal reality in the relation of the Father to the Son. Colossians 1:15 and Hebrews 1:3 both occur in a context that indicates that the Son was the image of God even prior to creation. Thus we can infer that when God made Adam and Eve in the image of God, their creation imitated an archetype. The archetype is found in the fact that the Son is the eternal image. Mankind is a derivative or ectypal image. Since human rationality is a gift of God, among many other gifts, it too is derivative. Human rationality reflects divine rationality. And the specific

way in which it reflects God is itself imitative of the reflection of the
Father in the Son, who is his image. (See fig. 3.4.)

Figure 3.4: Human Image of God Reflecting Divine Image in the Son

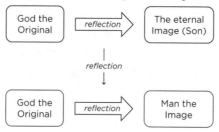

4

Implications of the Image of God

LET US CONSIDER further the implications of the idea of the image of God. We have said that the eternal Son, the second person of the Trinity, is the image of God (Col. 1:15). The relation between the Father and the Son is the archetypal case of imaging or reflection. But then also mankind is made in the image of God (Gen. 1:26–27). This nature of man reflects within the created order the archetypal image. It is an ectypal imaging or ectypal reflection. It is based on what is true within God himself, who is the archetype.

Analogy

What is the relation between archetype and ectype? In the case of human beings as ectypes, the archetype and the ectype are not on the same level. God is the Creator; human beings are creatures. Adam is *made in* the image of God; his being made implies that he is a creature. So we may say that he is the image of God on the level of the creature (1 Cor. 11:7). The second person of the Trinity *is* the image of God on the level of the Creator. They are not an image in exactly the same way. The second person of the Trinity is God, just as the Father is God. He is "the exact imprint of his [God's] nature" (Heb. 1:3). Adam is not God, and never will be. We might say that the Son is the *exact* image, while Adam is a derivative image.

But in addition to being derivative, Adam does not match God in everything. For example, God is omnipotent. Adam and his fellow human beings are given dominion (Gen. 1:28). This dominion implies that human beings have power and authority over the lower creation. But they are not omnipotent. Similarly, God is omniscient, while human beings have limited knowledge. (See fig. 4.1.)

Figure 4.1: Two Levels of Image

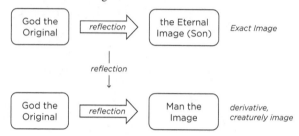

Let us describe the relation between God and man as a relation of *analogy*. God and man are not identical. But Adam is made in the image of God in a way that is *analogous* to the eternal Son being the image of God.

Figure 4.2: Two Analogies in the Language of Image of God

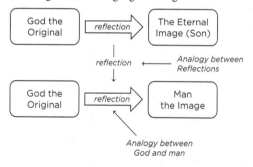

There are actually two distinct but related analogies. First, saying that Adam is made in the image of God implies that there is an analogy between God and man. Even more than the term *image*, the term *likeness* in Genesis 1:26 indicates an analogy between the two. Second, saying that the Son is the image of God implies that there is an analogy between two relations, the relation of the Father to the Son on the one hand and the relation between God and Adam on the other hand. Both are imaging relations or relations of reflection. (See fig. 4.2.)

Similarities and Differences

As a reference point, suppose that we consider an analogy between two distinct items. In Song of Solomon 2:1, the woman compares herself to "a rose of Sharon." There is an analogy between her and a rose. If we make a detailed comparison between her and the rose, we find that some things about the two are similar and other things are different.

We can see that the same pattern of similarity and difference occurs in both of the analogies above about God and human beings. God has power and human beings have power. This possession of power is a similarity. But God has all power, while human beings have limited power. So there is a difference. God speaks and then human beings speak. This ability to speak is a similarity. But God's speech is original and has the power to create light and other things. Human speech is derivative. By itself it does not "create" new objects in the world. This derivative character is a difference. (See fig. 4.3.)

Figure 4.3: Similarities and Differences in an Analogy

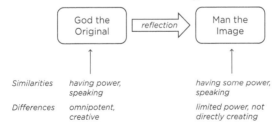

We can also see both similarity and difference in the two forms of reflection. The Son eternally reflects the Father. The relation between God and Adam is also a relation of reflection or imaging.

So there is a similarity. But there is also a difference. The Son is what he is eternally. The relation between God and Adam came into being only when God created Adam. The Son is the *exact* imprint of the Father, while Adam is, we might say, a kind of partial or analogical imprint.

We can also consider the idea of generation in the two cases. The Father eternally "begets" the Son, or fathers the Son. Eternal generation has been disputed in recent times, but it is acknowledged in the Nicene-Constantinopolitan Creed:

> We believe in . . . one Lord Jesus Christ, the Son of God, *the Only-begotten, Begotten of the Father* before all ages, Light of Light, Very God of Very God, *Begotten, not made*; of one essence with the Father; by whom all things were made.[1]

This eternal begetting is mysterious. The doctrine is justified by the fact that Jesus in his incarnation truly reveals God. That implies that there is a mysterious eternal background or archetype that is being reflected in the incarnation.[2]

The analogue within the created order is found in the fact that earthly fathers beget or father their sons. But this process takes place in time. It is *analogous* to, but distinct from, the eternal begetting of the Son.

We can see that there are some similarities, because we call both operations "begetting" or "fathering." But there is a distinction. The distinction is necessary in order to avoid the Arian heresy. The Arians falsely say that the Son came into being. They say that he came into being in the way that an earthly son comes into being. He is therefore only the highest and first creature. But this Arian idea is mistaken. The

---

1   The *Nicene-Constantinopolitan Creed*, https://orthodoxwiki.org/Nicene-Constantinopolitan _Creed, accessed April 11, 2020.

2   Vern S. Poythress, *Knowing and the Trinity: How Perspectives in Human Knowledge Imitate the Trinity* (Phillipsburg, NJ: P&R, 2018), ch. 24; Vern S. Poythress, *The Mystery of the Trinity: A Trinitarian Approach to the Attributes of God* (Phillipsburg, NJ: P&R, 2020), ch. 10.

mistake is in thinking that the begetting of the Son, an eternal begetting, is the same as the earthly begetting by an earthly father. They are analogous, but not the same. (See fig. 4.4.)

Figure 4.4: Similarities and Differences in Begetting

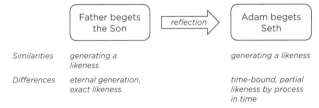

Similarities	*generating a likeness*	*generating a likeness*
Differences	*eternal generation, exact likeness*	*time-bound, partial likeness by process in time*

The Origin of Similarities and Differences in God

In discussing similarities and differences, we have mostly focused on the way in which similarities and differences work when we compare God and man. But now we should remember that the origin of this entire pattern lies in God. The Son is the "image of the invisible God" (Col. 1:15). The Son is God, fully God. The Father also is God. There is one God. This one divine nature is the "similarity" between the Father and the Son. We put "similarity" in quotes, because it is not a "mere" similarity, as if there were a distance between two separable things. There is only one "thing," namely God. So the similarity is a kind of identity, a deep unity.

But in addition to the similarity or identity, there is a distinction. The Son is not the Father. When we make this distinction, we affirm that there is a difference between the two persons. The difference is that one is the Son and the other is the Father. This way of describing the difference uses the analogy with a family, by using the terms *father* and *son*. But we can also use the analogy with communication. One person (the Father) is the speaker and the other (the Word) is the speech. Or we could use the analogy with reflections. One is the archetypal pattern and the other is the image of the pattern. All of this is mysterious.[3]

---

3   Poythress, *Knowing and the Trinity*, ch. 24.

There is no pattern within creation that could function as a model to dissolve the mystery. (See fig. 4.5.)

Figure 4.5: Similarity and Difference Applied to Father and Son in God

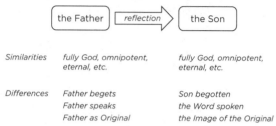

Similarities	fully God, omnipotent, eternal, etc.	fully God, omnipotent, eternal, etc.
Differences	Father begets Father speaks Father as Original	Son begotten the Word spoken the Image of the Original

Now, we know that God is absolute. He does not need any resources outside himself.[4] In particular, he does not need any extra resources in order to produce mankind, or to produce the analogies between himself and human beings. *Everything* has its source in him.

So the similarities and differences that we see in man being the image of God are similarities and differences that have their origin in God. He specifies them. They are derivative from God in a particular sense. The archetype for similarity and the archetype for difference are both found in God.

We have already seen how. The Son is "similar" to the Father and also "different" from the Father. We use quotation marks in both cases, because of the uniqueness of who God is. And yet it is appropriate to use some kind of terminology that indicates that the original unity in God and the original distinction in God (the distinctions among the persons) is the foundation for what we see when we look at Adam as the image of God, on the lower or derivative level of creaturely existence.

The Holy Spirit as a Person

So far in our discussion of similarity and difference, we have not explicitly mentioned the Holy Spirit. We might wonder how he is pertinent.

4   Poythress, *Mystery of the Trinity*, ch. 3.

We have not mentioned him up to this point because the explicit verses about the Son as image, namely Colossians 1:15 and Hebrews 1:3 (also 2 Cor. 4:6) do not explicitly mention the Holy Spirit.

The language of "image" is appropriately applied to the Son. In fact, sonship is closely related to image when we look at the human level:

> When Adam had lived 130 years, he fathered a *son* in his own *likeness*, after his *image*, and named him Seth. (Gen. 5:3)

In general, a son is in the image of his father. At the divine level, by analogy, the eternal Son is the image of his divine Father.

So does the Holy Spirit have any relation to the idea of image or reflection? The Holy Spirit was present during the whole process of creation in Genesis 1, as indicated by verse 2. Also, in the more specific description of the creation of Adam in 2:7, it says, "then the LORD God formed the man of dust from the ground and *breathed* into his nostrils the breath of life, and the man became a living creature." The act of breathing is reminiscent of the role of the Holy Spirit in some other cases: Ezekiel 37:9, 14; Psalm 104:29–30. And the Hebrew word for the Spirit, the word *ruach* (רוּחַ), can also mean "breath." The Holy Spirit is compared to the breath of God. We infer that the Holy Spirit was intimately involved in imparting breath and life to the man when God first created him, according to Genesis 2:7. We should also note that when God is about to create man, he speaks to himself, using the plural "us" and "our": "Let *us* make man in *our* image, after *our* likeness" (Gen. 1:26). Though the meaning of the plural is disputed, it seems best to take it as an early indication of plurality in God, the plurality of the persons of the Trinity. This verse is therefore a further evidence of the presence of the Holy Spirit with the other persons of the Trinity.

We have seen earlier that the Holy Spirit is compared to breath in the context of the analogy with communication. And the Holy Spirit is involved in the analogy with a family, since the eternal giving of the Holy Spirit is an expression of the love that the Father has for the Son (John 3:34–35). The three main analogies—the analogy with communication, the analogy with a family, and the analogy with reflections—express the same reality of the Trinity. Hence it is legitimate to infer that the Holy Spirit is involved also in the imaging or reflective relation between the Father and the Son. This pattern of reflections comes to manifestation in theophanies (appearances of God). When God appears in the Old Testament, it is the Father appearing through the Son. The Spirit is also present, in association with the glory of God.[5]

As in the case of the analogy with a family, the Holy Spirit functions in the bond relating one person to another. The Holy Spirit as the expression of love expresses the bond between the Father and the Son in the analogy with a family. As the expression of the glory of God, he also expresses the bond between the Father and the Son in theophany. The glory displayed in the Son reflects the glory of the Father. The Holy Spirit also expresses the bond between God and the human person who sees a theophany. The Holy Spirit as the expression of the presence of God is immediately present to the person who is the recipient of a theophany.

The final "theophany" takes place in the incarnate Christ. Christ is "God with us" (Matt. 1:23). His presence through his human nature is permanent, unlike the temporary appearances of God in the Old Testament. The temporary appearances in the Old Testament foreshadow this final, permanent appearance in the New Testament.[6] In the New Testament, it becomes clear that the Holy Spirit is the immediate agent through whom we are united to Christ, and through whom the Father and the Son make their home in each of us (John 14:16–17, 23).

Thus, we can see that the Holy Spirit is preeminently the one who brings the Son into relation to us. More broadly, the Holy Spirit func-

---

5   Vern S. Poythress, *Theophany: A Biblical Theology of God's Appearing* (Wheaton, IL: Crossway, 2018), chs. 16–17; Poythress, *Knowing and the Trinity*, 71–75.

6   Poythress, *Theophany*, 19–24.

tions in personal relations. So the *relation* of analogy between God and man is a relation mediated by the Holy Spirit and associated with the Holy Spirit. The Holy Spirit may also be correlated to the *relation* between the Father and the Son, as expressed in the Father's love for the Son. The Holy Spirit is intimately involved in these relations, which we have seen are relations of analogy.

The Three Persons as Archetypal Pattern for Analogy

In the Trinity, each of the three persons is God, as we have noted. But it is also true that each person is distinct from the other two and each person has a preeminent function with respect to the nature of analogy, as we have described it.

First, God the Father preeminently represents the *unity* of God. He is called simply "God" without a further description (John 20:17; 2 Cor. 13:14). And the expression "Son of God" gives the name "God" to the Father, who is the Father of the Son.

Second, God the Son is begotten by the Father, as confirmed by the fact that he is called the "Son." He is preeminently involved in this differentiation and distinction between the person of the Father and the person of the Son. So he preeminently represents the archetype for *differentiation* or distinction.

Third, the Holy Spirit, as we have seen, preeminently expresses the harmony in relations in God, including the relation between the Father and the Son.[7] (See table 4.1 and fig. 4.6.)

Table 4.1: The Trinitarian Source for Unity and Distinction

God the Father	*God the Son*	*God the Holy Spirit*
preeminent in unity	preeminent in distinction	preeminent in harmony in relations

---

7 Poythress, *Mystery of the Trinity*, ch. 13; Poythress, *Knowing and the Trinity*, appendix F.

Figure 4.6: The Trinitarian Source for Unity and Distinction

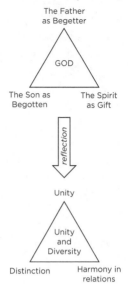

Analogy, we have said, involves both similarity and difference. The similarity that belongs to an analogy is a reflection of the unity that is in God. This unity is represented by God the Father. The difference that belongs to an analogy is a reflection of the diversity that is in God. This diversity is represented preeminently by God the Son. Finally, the analogy itself, as a multifaceted relation, is a reflection of the Holy Spirit, who preeminently expresses relations. (See table 4.2 and fig. 4.7.)

Table 4.2: The Trinitarian Source for Analogy

God the Father	God the Son	God the Holy Spirit
reflected preeminently in similarities	reflected preeminently in differences	reflected preeminently in analogy

This triad, consisting in similarities, differences, and a relation, belongs intrinsically to analogy. It belongs first to the archetypal analogy between the Father and the Son. And then, as reflection, it belongs derivatively to the analogy between God and mankind. We take note of this analogy when we affirm that mankind is made "in the image of God" (Gen. 1:27).

Figure 4.7: The Trinitarian Source for Analogy

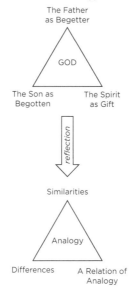

Coinherence

We may also bring into our discussion the biblical teaching about *indwelling*. We know from the doctrine of the Trinity that the persons of the Trinity indwell each other (see John 17:21–23; 14:23).[8] This mutual indwelling is called *coinherence*. Now, the triad for analogy, consisting in similarities, differences, and a relation, is a triad reflecting the persons of the Trinity. So does it also reflect the coinherence of the persons?

It does. The archetypal coinherence is of course the coinherence of the persons. But this archetype may be *reflected*, just as the image of God in the Son is reflected in the image of God in man. (See fig. 4.8.)

---

8   Poythress, *Knowing and the Trinity*, ch. 7; Poythress, *Mystery of the Trinity*, ch. 11.

Figure 4.8: Coinherence Reflected in Aspects of Analogy

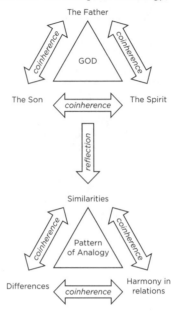

The reflection would mean that the three aspects—that is, similarity, difference, and analogy—are interlocked. They involve each other. Each, when further examined, implies the other two. Let us see how this might work.

First, let us see how similarities imply differences. The pattern of similarities in an analogy, such as the image of God in man, implies also differences. The similarities are not a monadic identity. An analogy is usually not an analogy *only* at one isolated point, but consists in a *pattern* of similarities. So each point of similarity can also be seen to differ from other points of similarity. For example, Adam is similar to Seth in that both are made in the image of God, and also because Seth is in the image of Adam and reflects Adam. This similarity probably included ways in which Seth physically looked like Adam. But it also includes the many features that belong in common to human nature in general. Seth has the ability to speak, to plan, to worship, to be in communion with other persons.

Conversely, the pattern of differences implies the existence of similarities alongside the differences. We cannot have a difference without some understanding of a feature of one side of the analogy that differs from a feature on other side. And yet the differences, to be meaningful, must belong together within a larger whole. For example, Adam differs from his son Seth, and any difference that Adam has, such as being the first father, is understandable because we understand the broader category of "father." Adam is similar to all other fathers.

The similarities and differences belong together within a larger whole, namely the relation of analogy. So the existence of analogy implies similarities and differences, and conversely similarities and differences together imply analogy.

Perspectives on Language: Contrast, Variation, and Distribution

The triad consisting in similarities, differences, and the relation of analogy has an affinity to another triad previously developed in the study of language. It is the triad consisting in three aspects belonging to any unit of language: (1) contrastive-identificational features; (2) variation; and (3) distribution.[9] (See fig. 4.9.)

As an illustration within the realm of language, consider the word *horse* and its meaning. *Horse* is distinct from other words, and has its own identity. It has a particular spelling and a particular meaning. This particular identity—and the features that aid us in discerning that identity—is what is described with the term *contrastive-identificational features*, or *contrast* for short. The word *horse* also has a range of pronunciations, in the form of slight variations, and it has a variation in meaning in that it appropriately applies to a variety of horses of different ages and breeds. This range is what is termed *variation*. Finally, the *distribution* of the word is the range of contexts in which it is expected

9   Poythress, *Knowing and the Trinity*, appendix F; Poythress, *Mystery of the Trinity*, ch. 13; Kenneth L. Pike, *Linguistic Concepts: An Introduction to Tagmemics* (Lincoln, NB/London: University of Nebraska Press, 1982), chs. 6–8; Vern S. Poythress, "Reforming Ontology and Logic in the Light of the Trinity: An Application of Van Til's Idea of Analogy," *Westminster Theological Journal* 57 (1995): 187–219.

to appear or in which it appropriately appears. As a noun, it fits into noun phrases, which in turn fit into whole clauses and sentences. In meaning, it designates horses who engage in various kinds of activity.

Figure 4.9: The Triad for Analogy and the Triad for Units of Language

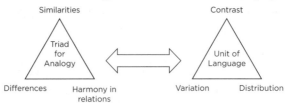

The first aspect, *contrast*, has an affinity with the elements of *similarity* in an analogy. Similarities, including specific features, are what enable us to identify the word *horse* as the *same* word in each new occurrence. The new occurrence is *similar* at appropriate points to the earlier occurrences. The same goes for actual horses out in the world. We identify a new specimen as a horse because it has features *similar* to the features of other horses with which we have had experience.

The second aspect, *variation*, has an affinity with the elements of *difference* in an analogy. An analogy holds because the similarities continue across a mental space where there is variation in what we are looking at. In the analogy between Adam and his son Seth, the variation consists in the fact that Adam and Seth are variant instances of humanity. They are also two variant instances of the pattern of similarity that they share.

The third aspect, *distribution*, has an affinity with the relation of analogy as a whole. Distribution represents the *context* in which a word like *horse* occurs. Similarly, the analogy as a whole is the context in which the similarities and differences occur.

Now, contrast, variation, and distribution are correlated respectively with the Father, the Son, and the Spirit.[10] This correlation confirms

---

10 Poythress, *Knowing and the Trinity*, appendix F. The correlation between the Trinity and the triad for contrast, variation, and distribution is in fact much like what we have ob-

our observations above about the way in which Father, Son, and Spirit preeminently express the themes of similarity, difference, and relation within analogy.

Analogy in General

We have focused on the key archetypal case of analogy, namely the analogy between the Father and the Son. And then we have seen that an analogy is present in the truth that mankind is made in the image of God. Both of these instances of analogy harmonize with a broader use of the term *analogy* in the English language. The *Merriam-Webster* on-line dictionary has the following as the first sense of the word *analogy*:

> **1 a** : a comparison of two otherwise unlike things based on resemblance of a particular aspect
> **b** : resemblance in some particulars between things otherwise unlike : SIMILARITY[11]

Both definitions in *Merriam-Webster*, 1a and 1b, discuss similarity and difference. They both have the term *resemblance*, indicating a similarity, and the term *unlike*, indicating difference. 1a seems to emphasize the difference, by putting "otherwise unlike things" near the beginning in its wording. 1b seems to emphasize the similarity, by putting the word *resemblance* near the beginning and by concluding with the near-synonym *similarity*. But it is a matter of emphasis whether we focus on the similarities or the differences. Both are there.

Both definitions 1a and 1b may also imply a relation. In 1a, "comparison" involves a relation between the two things being compared. In 1b, "resemblance" is "in some particulars," typically more than one particular feature, so that the situation involves a larger structure of

---

served in earlier paragraphs in the present chapter. The Father preeminently represents the unity of God, and hence whatever contrastive-identificational features identify him as God. And likewise with variation and distribution.

11   *Merriam-Webster* online dictionary, https://www.merriam-webster.com/dictionary /analogy, accessed April 11, 2020.

similarity. And that structure involves a relation between the two things.[12]

So the *Merriam-Webster* definitions are in line with our analysis of analogy in terms of three aspects, namely similarity, difference, and a relation. The last of these, the relation, is the same as the analogy itself.

12 J. F. Ross, *Portraying Analogy* (Cambridge: Cambridge University Press, 1981), 87, in discussing word meanings, distinguishes "similarity" from "relatedness." Word meanings can exhibit some similarity ("semantic overlap") without being "related." It seems to me that Ross's idea of "relatedness" is akin to what we have in mind in cases where two items participate in a larger structure of similarities.

PART II

ANALOGY

We consider the nature of analogy.

5

The Nature of Analogy in Thought

NOW LET US BEGIN to focus specifically on human thought and reasoning.

Archetypal and Ectypal Thought

We have a key to understanding the origin of human thought. God's thoughts are the archetype. Human thoughts are ectypal reflections of divine thoughts. Isaiah 55:8–9 is relevant:

> For my thoughts are not your thoughts,
>> neither are your ways my ways, declares the LORD.
> For as the heavens are higher than the earth,
>> so are my ways higher than your ways
>> and my thoughts than your thoughts.

These verses emphasize the *distinction* between God's thoughts and those of Israel. But the use of the word *thoughts* still shows an element of similarity. We have already seen that the creation of mankind in the image of God invites us to look for similarities between God and man. And this is one of them. We as human beings have thoughts because, first of all, there is an archetype for thinking in God. (See fig. 2.6.)

Since there is both similarity and difference between God's thoughts and human thoughts, we can say that there is an *analogy* between the two levels. The human level reflects the divine level.

We have also seen that the pattern of reflections is repeated. At the archetypal level, the Son is the image of the Father. He reflects the Father. Adam as an image of God reflects God, and therefore also reflects the Son of God. Adam in turn fathers Seth, who is "a son in his own likeness, after his image" (Gen. 5:3). Seth reflects Adam.

If the pattern of reflection occurs more than once, at different levels and at different points, does the same re-occurrence take place with respect to *thoughts*? Does re-occurrence take place with respect to *analogy*? In particular, is one human thought analogous to another? Human thought imitates divine thought. And divine thought includes reflection, in that the Son reflects the Father. The Father knows the Son, and also the Son knows the Father (Matt. 11:27). So does human thought include within it ectypal cases of reflection and analogy?

Personal Perspectives

We may make a step toward an answer by considering the role of perspectives. The word *perspective* can include the connotation of *limitation*. Any one human being is finite, and has a limited perspective on the totality of knowledge. Clearly, divine thought is not limited. So divine thought cannot be perspectival in this way. But divine thought is personal. As indicated in the preceding paragraph, the Father knows the Son. The Father has a personal perspective, as the Father, in his knowledge. And his knowledge has a particular focus on the object of knowledge, namely the Son. In this sense, the Father has a personal perspective as a knower. Likewise, the Son has a personal perspective. He knows all things *as the Son*. The Holy Spirit has a personal perspective, in that he "searches everything, even the depths of God" (1 Cor. 2:10).[1] These three modes of knowledge differ in their personal starting point. Within the Trinity, each person agrees with the other two in the content of knowledge. Each person knows comprehensively all that God

---

1   Vern S. Poythress, *Knowing and the Trinity: How Perspectives in Human Knowledge Imitate the Trinity* (Phillipsburg, NJ: P&R, 2018), ch. 30; Vern S. Poythress, *The Mystery of the Trinity: A Trinitarian Approach to the Attributes of God* (Phillipsburg, NJ: P&R, 2020), ch. 47.

knows, and God knows everything (1 John 3:20; 1 Cor. 2:10). When we compare the three modes of knowing, we see both agreement and difference. This combination of agreement and difference is an archetype for the existence of analogy at the human level.

At the human level, each of us has his or her own personal perspective. One person's knowledge overlaps with another's, but there are also differences in texture, due to the uniqueness of each person. The differences among the four Gospels constitute one important illustration. Each human writer of one of the Gospels has some distinct emphases.[2]

In this way, humanity imitates the unity and diversity of the Trinity. Human knowledge is in part shared. This unity in knowledge imitates the unity in the Trinity. At the same time, each person has a distinct personal perspective on his knowledge. His knowledge in its personal orientation is distinct from the knowledge of other human beings. Bob's knowledge is *Bob's*. And Alice's knowledge is *Alice's*. This distinction between human persons reflects the distinction in persons in the Trinity.

The combination of similarity and difference between two people's knowledge enables us to say that the knowledge by one is *analogous* to the knowledge by the other. Sharing of knowledge is possible because two people are similar in being human beings and being made in the image of God.

Perspectives and Analogy

In fact, there is a close relation between perspectives and analogy. Let us consider two personal perspectives on an object of knowledge—say, a pet rabbit. Alice and Barbara each have a perspective on the rabbit. Their knowledge overlaps, and that constitutes the similarity. The two persons are distinct, and that constitutes the difference. The knowledge of one person is analogous to the knowledge of the other. (See fig. 5.1.)

---

2   Vern S. Poythress, *Symphonic Theology: The Validity of Multiple Perspectives in Theology* (repr., Phillipsburg, NJ: P&R, 2001), 47–51.

Figure 5.1: Alice's Knowledge and Barbara's

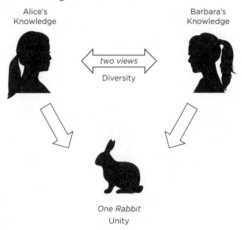

We can also consider the similarities and differences between two *thematic* perspectives.[3] Let us consider Alice. At one time she considers her pet rabbit from the perspective of care. She thinks about what goes into caring for her rabbit. At another time she considers her rabbit from the perspective of artistry. Is her rabbit beautiful? What artistic characteristics might she find in her present view of her rabbit or in a photograph that she might take in order to have a permanent record? The two thematic perspectives overlap, because they are focused on the same object, namely the rabbit. But they also differ. So they are analogous to each other.

We can also see that there is a form of analogy built into even a single perspective. A perspective may be defined as a view of something from somewhere by someone.[4] More specifically, it is an *analogical* view of something. Analogy is built in. If, for example, Alice is considering her rabbit using an artistic perspective, she is exploiting the fact that there is analogy between her previous experiences and sense of artistry on the one hand and the rabbit on the other hand. A thematic perspective, by applying a particular theme like the theme of artistry to a new object

---

3   On thematic perspectives, see Poythress, *Knowing and the Trinity*, chs. 4, 31.
4   Poythress, *Knowing and the Trinity*, ch. 29.

(her rabbit), involves at least minimally the use of an analogy between the new object and previous knowledge. In this case, the previous knowledge is knowledge of artistry. (See fig. 5.2.)

Figure 5.2: Analogy in a Perspective

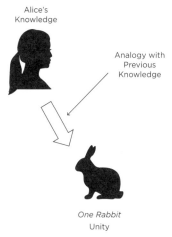

Alice's
Knowledge

Analogy with
Previous
Knowledge

One Rabbit
Unity

Analogy operates in a perspective because the perspective treats an object from a particular viewpoint, and that viewpoint depends on the evocation of analogy in some form.

With a thematic perspective, such as the artistic perspective, the analogy exists between the object analyzed (the rabbit) and previous ideas of artistry. With a personal perspective, such as Alice's perspective on the rabbit, the main analogy is the analogy between the entirety of Alice's previous personal experience on the one hand and the rabbit on the other hand.

There is also a third kind of perspective, a spatial perspective.[5] This kind of perspective is in some respects the easiest. Alice sees her rabbit from the standpoint of her present location in space. Depending on her location and on the orientation of the rabbit, she might see only the rabbit's right side, or only its face and the front part of its body, or only its back. In this case, the main analogy is an analogy between the

5   Poythress, *Knowing and the Trinity*, ch. 2.

two-dimensional perception of the rabbit (with some sense of depth due to binocular vision) and the three-dimensional reality of the rabbit. The three-dimensional reality is not fully visible from any one location by the observer. Rather, Alice combines knowledge acquired from variations in spatial location. The temporary two-dimensional experience has both similarities and differences in comparison with the in-depth knowledge that Alice obtains by synthesizing all possible spatial views of the rabbit.

6

Analogy as a Perspective
on Classification

WE HAVE SEEN that the archetype for analogy is to be found in the Trinity, in the unity and diversity of persons and the unity and diversity of personal knowledge. We also know that God is simple. That means that he is indecomposable.[1] His attributes are not separable, but rather they interpenetrate. In fact, the interpenetration of attributes within the Trinity reflects the interpenetration of the persons in their mutual indwelling (coinherence).[2] This interpenetration must extend to all features about God, including the presence of analogy. So analogy is a perspective on everything in God.

Since all truth has its archetype in God's knowledge, truth is interpenetrated by analogy. Thus it is fitting to use analogy (as well as any attribute of God) as a perspective on all truth.[3]

---

1 Vern S. Poythress, *The Mystery of the Trinity: A Trinitarian Approach to the Attributes of God* (Phillipsburg, NJ: P&R, 2020), ch. 9; Vern S. Poythress, *Knowing and the Trinity: How Perspectives in Human Knowledge Imitate the Trinity* (Phillipsburg, NJ: P&R, 2018), chs. 33–34.

2 Poythress, *Mystery of the Trinity*, ch. 31.

3 C. S. Lewis comes near to this view, as he reflects on metaphor (a form of analogy): "all our truth, or all but a few fragments, is won by metaphor" ("Bluspels and Flalansferes: A Semantic Nightmare," in *Selected Literary Essays*, 265, ed. Walter Hooper [Cambridge: Cambridge University Press, 1969]).

As we observed earlier, all human thought is an analogical imitation of God's knowledge of the truth. So all human thought is analogical in this sense. But does human thought rely on internal analogies between its various aspects? Our exploration of perspectives in the preceding chapter suggests that it does. And this exploration is confirmed by the observation that whenever we have access to truth of any kind, this truth is suitably viewed using a perspective involving analogy.

Let us consider some instances of the use of analogy.

Analogy in Classification

First, analogy is used in one of the most basic operations of human thought, namely classification. Is Fido a dog? We will judge that he is a dog if he is like dogs in a sufficiently robust way. That likeness between Fido and other dogs is a form of analogy. (See fig. 6.1.)

Figure 6.1: Classifying by Analogy

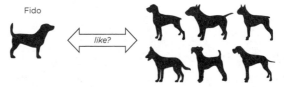

When we learn a new word, the new word is a kind of classification. We may picture a child learning the word *horse*. He does it not by having a premade exact concept from the beginning, but by making observations about things that are called horses, and by seeing an analogy between any two examples that he has. Perhaps he also receives some additional hints or guidance from a parent or teacher, who tells him to notice that each horse has four feet and a head and a tail. Animals of other kinds also have four feet and a head and a tail. So then the teacher tells him to notice the size of the horse and the shape of the head and the hooves on the feet.

So what happens when the child sees a new horse that he has never seen before? There is not an exact match with any of the previous horses. So he has to go partly by analogies with the previous horses, and analogies that he has already noticed among various animals that he has been told previously are horses. When we ourselves craft for ourselves a new kind of classification, whether for a new species of animal or a new classification of paintings or ideas or furniture, we create the classification partly because we see notable analogies between the individual things or individual ideas. If someone proposes to include a new instance in our classification, we have to decide whether the new instance is sufficiently analogous in the appropriate ways.

We use analogy in typical cases of classifying, because the class has a fuzzy boundary. There are some cases that we confidently classify as horses, and other cases that we confidently classify as something else—a donkey, perhaps. But are there cases that are more difficult, cases that make us feel that we cannot draw the line precisely? For a young child, the class of horses still has a somewhat fuzzy boundary. He is still in the process of learning where to draw the line. And when a new classification is invented, the boundary may not be precisely defined. There is some flux. (See fig. 6.2.)

Figure 6.2: Fuzzy Boundary in Classification

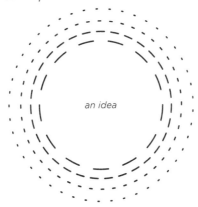

an idea

Analogy in Extreme Cases

We can consider an extreme case where it is alleged that we do not use analogy. Let us suppose that we have a precisely delineated list of features that make something a member of the species *Equus ferus* (the species of domestic horses). Because the list is precise, it might seem that we have avoided any use of analogy. But the precise list is the result of a refinement that depended on numerous observations of analogies. They should be called analogies because every individual horse is different. And every individual horse is also similar to other horses.

Once we have the refined list, we still have to judge whether a particular individual animal has the features belonging to the list. One of the features might be hooves with a certain shape. Then we have to make a judgment as to whether that sort of hoof belongs to the new animal that we are considering. And that judgment still relies on analogy. Is the hoof feature of our new animal sufficiently analogous to other animals that have this defining feature? To avoid analogy, we might try to refine our definition of the one feature, perhaps calling it "hooves of a certain shape." But then we would produce something like a refined list of characteristics that are the defining characteristics of hooves. We are just pushing the difficulty back.

For example, we may push back the difficulty in defining *horse* by going from the word *horse* to the more refined concept *Equus ferus*. And then we push the difficulty back again, by moving from the expression *Equus ferus* to a list of features. And then for each feature we move to the defining characteristics of that feature. We ourselves always take up a position at the end of the process, so to speak. *We* have to make a personal judgment as to whether a particular characteristic belongs to a new case. In our personal reckoning, we are still using analogy.[4]

---

4   See a similar issue in the challenge of applying rigorous logic to cases in the wide world (Vern S. Poythress, "Semiotic Analysis of Symbolic Logic Using Tagmemic Theory: With Implications for Analytic Philosophy," *Semiotica*, 2021, https://doi.org/10.1515/sem -2020-0018, https://frame-poythress.org/a-semiotic-analysis-of-symbolic-logic-using -tagmemic-theory-with-implications-for-analytic-philosophy/); Vern S. Poythress, A Semiotic Analysis of Multiple Systems of Logic: Using Tagmemic Theory to Assess the Usefulness and Limitations of Formal Logics, and to Produce a Mathematical Lattice Model Including Multiple Systems of Logic," *Semiotica* 2021 (January 2022), doi.org/10.1515/ sem-2020-0051, https://frame-poythress.org/a-semiotic-analysis-of-multiple-systems-of -logic-using-tagmemic-theory-to-assess-the-usefulness-and-limitations-of-formal-logics -and-to-produce-a-mathematical-lattice-model-including-multiple-systems-of-logic/.

Could we escape by appealing to the genetic information in the DNA inside the cells of horses? But that information differs slightly from one horse to another, because of mutations and natural variations in the information from the previous generations. How different does it have to be before we think we no longer have a horse? In the end, we have to make a judgment. The judgment involves a decision concerning the analogy between the information in the DNA of one cell and the information in the DNA from another cell.

7

Analogy in the Three
Fundamental Laws of Logic

WE MAY CONSIDER how analogy functions in the "three fundamental laws of logic." According to the *Encyclopedia Britannica*, the three fundamental laws of logic are "(1) the law of contradiction, (2) the law of excluded middle (or excluded third), and (3) the principle of identity."[1] Let us consider these three laws one at a time. We begin with the third principle, which is in some ways the most basic.

The Principle of Identity

We begin with the principle of identity. The principle of identity has more than one alternate formulation. One formulation is, "a thing is identical with itself." (See fig. 7.1.)

This principle may seem to be straightforward and without difficulty. But it can be considered as a form of classification, in which the class consists of only one thing. If we look at the same thing a second time, we have to be able to see whether it is genuinely the same thing. Does it belong to the class consisting of the one thing that we previously singled out? That is not always easy to decide. Has someone secretly substituted one tennis ball for another or one marble for another while we were out of the room?

---

1   *Encyclopedia Britannica*, https://www.britannica.com/topic/laws-of-thought, accessed April 14, 2020. The law of contradiction is sometimes called the law of *non*contradiction, as we have designated it up to this point. Hereafter, we will refer to it as the law of contradiction.

Figure 7.1: The Law of Identity

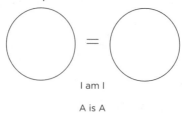

I am I

A is A

I am myself, am I not?

To avoid difficulties of this kind, the principle of identity might be further refined by saying that it applies only to a single thing at one instant of time. In this interpretation, the principle allows that things may change over time, and that one thing can change into something else. It also allows for people to be mistaken about identity, as in a case where one tennis ball is substituted for another.

Yet the subjective aspect of judgments about identity remains. At a later time, we have a memory of the tennis ball that we saw earlier. What we remember, we remember about the *same* tennis ball that we saw. The memory refers to the same ball. The memory ball is identical with the actual ball. Or is it? Someone's memory may be faulty. He or she may confuse one memory with another. In the case of memory, we are in fact using an analogy between the memory and the actual ball. (See fig. 7.2.)

Figure 7.2: Memory of a Ball

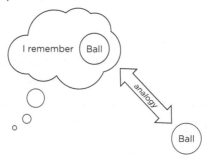

To escape the use of analogy, we could try to do what we did earlier with the concept of a horse. We can try refining our concept. So now, the concept of the "identity" of a thing is refined until it is an instantaneous snapshot of the tennis ball. It is neither an analogical comparison between two different times at which the ball exists, nor an analogical comparison between a memory and the real thing, but it is an instantaneous observation. That observation is what it is. It is identical with itself. But the only way that we have of thinking about the observation and talking about the observation is by using words that endure over time and memories that endure over time. The instantaneous observation is a kind of ideal that we can never really grasp and master, because it does not stay with us. As soon as we think we have it, it is gone.

The principle of identity is of practical use only if we can apply it to everyday life. And it can apply there because we recognize continuity in time. The tennis ball continues to sit on the floor from one moment to the next. Even if it is being batted back and forth on a tennis court, we perceive the continuity in its existence. It is identical with itself *over time*. We can make similar observations concerning our memories and our powers of classification. They endure over time.

But this endurance over time has complexities. It is not a perfectly static endurance in the form of complete unchangeability. As the tennis ball is batted back and forth, gradually and imperceptibly it is losing a few strands of fuzz that belonged to it when it was first taken from a newly opened canister. We detect the identity of the tennis ball alongside of change—alongside of variation. Using the analysis from chapter 4 above, we may observe that the tennis ball as a perceptible, meaningful thing has contrast, variation, and distribution. So does any particular person's concept of the tennis ball.

The principle of identity is one expression of the principle of *contrast*. Each thing is itself, with features that identify it. These features are contrastive-identificational features that also serve to contrast it with other things. It contrasts with other tennis balls, with soccer balls, with baseballs, with footballs, with marbles, and with many other kinds of things. The aspects of contrast interlock with the aspects of variation and distribution. (See fig. 7.3.)

Figure 7.3: Identity through Contrast

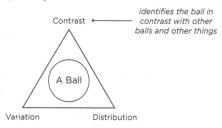

As we saw before, these three aspects—contrast, variation, and distribution—are together a reflection of the Trinity. One tennis ball is mysterious, in a manner that reflects the Trinity. It follows that the principle of identity, or the principle of contrast, is mysterious.

The Law of Excluded Middle

The second fundamental law of logic is the law of excluded middle. This law says that, for any particular proposition, such as the proposition that snow is white, either the proposition or its negation is true. Either snow is white, or snow is not white. (See fig. 7.4.)

Figure 7.4: The Law of Excluded Middle

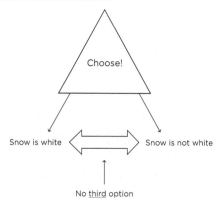

This principle is dependent on the use of variation. "Snow is white" and "snow is not white" are two distinct propositions. Each contrasts with the other. But in addition to contrast, there is variation when we compare the two. We can see this truth if we start with elements of commonality between the two propositions. Both propositions are propositions; both are about snow; they both say something about the color of snow; and both contain a reference to the color white. In addition to all these commonalities, there is variation. They are two cases belonging to the larger category of statements about snow. The two instances are variations within this larger category. (See fig. 7.5.)

Figure 7.5: Variation in Options

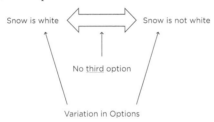

To understand the law of excluded middle, we must have an appreciation for the phenomenon of variation. And, as we saw earlier, variation interlocks with contrast and distribution. In this case, the distribution is partly the distribution of a context of many other propositions of all kinds. But there is also a kind of distribution in the world, in the sense that there is a world in which snow exists. Any particular bit of snow exists at a particular time and place within the world, and its environment in the world is an instance of distribution.

As usual, there is mystery in the interlocking of contrast, variation, and distribution. This mystery is derived from the Trinity. In the case of the law of excluded middle, the most prominent mystery is the mystery of variation. We have two related propositions, belonging to a single larger category. And we are told that we must choose one.

Only one is true. There is no middle ground. If it is not true that snow is not white, it must be true that snow is white. These two possibilities together are the two "variations" in possibilities for propositions and for truths about the world.

Variation enters our discussion in another way. There is variation in the meaning of the word *white* and variation in the word *snow*. What counts as "white"? Would something that is a little off-white, with a little grayishness to it, still count as white? Is a dirty snowball still an instance of snow? What if a mound of snow has partially melted and partially refrozen? Maybe we can find portions that are a bit icy and that look partially transparent, perhaps with a bit of blue. Is refrozen snow still snow?

So now, is the middle actually "excluded"? The "middle" would be a third proposition between "snow is white" and "snow is not white." Maybe we want to say in a particular case, "this snow is kind-of white." We experience a fuzzy boundary. And fuzzy boundaries are instances where variation is at work. If our propositions were a perfect ideal, we might say, there would be no middle ground. Then have we made the law true by artificially excluding anything that would make it not true?

Figure 7.6: Dirty Snow

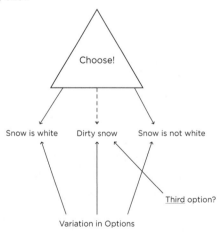

Putting it that way, with the word "artificially," makes it sound as though the presence of two exclusive options is a complete fiction. But in practice, in real life, even though there is some fuzziness, we often find ourselves in a position where we have to make binary choices. So the law of excluded middle is not artificial. But neither is it a guideline that has no practical limits. Sometimes snow is dirty. (See fig. 7.6.)

The Law of Contradiction

The third fundamental law is the law of contradiction (or, *non*contradiction, as we have called it). This law says that two contradictory propositions cannot both be true.[2] For example, it cannot be the case both that snow is white and that snow is not white. This formula sounds a little like the law of excluded middle. But there is a distinction between the two laws. The law of excluded middle says that there is no *third* option; if you do not choose one option, you are forced to the second. On the other hand, the law of contradiction says that if you *do* choose one option, you cannot simultaneously choose the second, the one that contradicts the first. The two laws make opposite points. The law of excluded middle focuses on our inability to create a space or separation between the two poles, in order to find a third option. The law forbids separation. By contrast, the law of contradiction focuses on our inability to smash the two poles together by holding them both to be true. The law forbids improper union or unity. (See fig. 7.7.)

This law of contradiction is a principle of logical harmony. Truth is coherent. Each true proposition fits within a larger whole, harmonizing with other true propositions. Even before we survey the whole field of true propositions, we know already that we will never find a proposition that is true and that is in disharmony (contradiction) with some other true proposition.

---

2   On the difficulty with the context-free notion of a "proposition," see Vern S. Poythress, *Logic: A God-Centered Approach to the Foundation of Western Thought* (Wheaton, IL: Crossway, 2013), chs. 17–21; Vern S. Poythress, "Reformed Ontology and Logic in the Light of the Trinity: An Application of Van Til's Idea of Analogy," *Westminster Theological Journal* 57 (1995): 187–219.

Figure 7.7: The Law of Contradiction

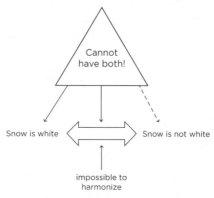

How do we know that? We might say we know it intuitively, as a basic insight or a basic assumption. We know it because if it were not true, all reasoning would be at an end. But our intuitions, our insights, and our assumptions are not independent insights that we have because each of us is allegedly a god. We reflect God. God is the origin of harmony and the origin of truth. The argument for the impossibility of the opposite, the argument that otherwise all reasoning would be at an end, is itself derivative from the archetypal wisdom of God. The person who would destroy harmony in God would destroy God. That is not possible. But if it were possible, that would be the end, not only of all reasoning, but of all existence.

Harmony is preeminently a relation. And so it leads to reflection on the idea of *distribution*. Each truth is distributed in relation to other truths, as well as falsehoods. The reality that contradictory statements cannot both be true is a reality about a pattern of relationships. In this pattern, each proposition is set over against the proposition that is its negation. The pattern of relations is a pattern of distribution.[3] As usual, distribution exists in interlocking relation to contrast and variation. This interlocking has in back of it the reality of the Trinity. It reflects

---

3   More specifically, it is a pattern of "distribution as a point in a system" (Kenneth L. Pike, *Linguistic Concepts: An Introduction to Tagmemics* [Lincoln/London: University of Nebraska Press, 1982], 65).

the Trinity. The law of contradiction preeminently expresses a reality concerning the third aspect in the interlocking, the aspect of distribution. (See fig. 7.8.)

Figure 7.8: The Law of Contradiction Related to Distribution

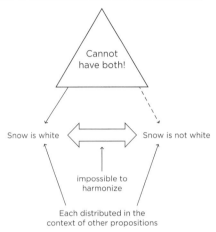

The Dependence of the Three Laws of Logic

The three fundamental laws of logic have a relation to the three aspects of units in language, that is, the aspects of contrast, variation, and distribution. Each one of the laws preeminently manifests *one* aspect in more prominence. The principle of identity manifests contrast (abbreviated as *C*). The law of excluded middle manifests variation (abbreviated as *V*). And the law of contradiction manifests distribution (abbreviated as *D*). Contrast, variation, and distribution interlock (in shorthand, CVD). So likewise, the three laws interlock. (See fig. 7.9.)

We cannot actually have one of the three (CVD) without tacitly depending on the other two. For example, the principle of identity affirms the self-identity of each truth. This ball is this ball. Its identity is in *contrast* with other balls and other kinds of objects. The self-identity of the ball is actually identifiable in relation to variations—various other possibilities. And its meaning implies the denial of its contradictory (its opposite). This particular object cannot be a ball and also not be a ball. The law of excluded middle presupposes the self-identity of each of the two alternatives contemplated. A ball is a ball, and also something that is not a ball is not a ball. And to say that one of the alternatives must be chosen is also to know tacitly that the contradictory proposition, that neither must be chosen, must be rejected. The law of contradiction presupposes the self-identity of each of the two propositions that are the negations of each other. And it presupposes that each of the two propositions is a proposition that is a distinct variation within the larger category, "a proposition taken together with its negation."

Figure 7.9: Three Laws of Logic Related to Contrast, Variation, and Distribution

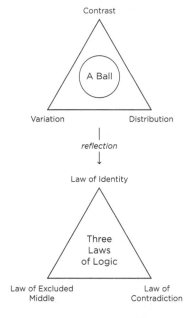

Thus, the three laws of logic are expressions respectively of the three aspects of meaningful units, the aspects of contrast, variation, and distribution. These three aspects in turn are reflections of the three persons of the Trinity. The laws of logic reflect the Trinity. (See table 7.1.)

Table 7.1: The Laws of Logic and the Trinity

The Trinity	Meaningful Units	Laws of Logic
Father	contrast	principle of identity
Son	variation	law of excluded middle
Holy Spirit	distribution	law of contradiction

Now consider again how the three laws of logic reflect the Trinity.

The Father is identical with himself. This is the foundation for the principle of identity.

The Son is distinct from the Father. In the relation of Father to Son, there are two persons. One chooses to focus either on the Father or on the One begotten of the Father. The Son is the foundation for the law of excluded middle.

The Holy Spirit is the bond of harmony. His expression of harmony within the Trinity is the foundation for the law of contradiction. The law of contradiction says that truth is harmonious. Therefore there are no genuine contradictions in the truth.

The three laws of logic also reflect the *mystery* of the Trinity. The laws are not, as many people suppose, transparent and nonmysterious. They are not laws that we *master*.

A Christian Conception of the Three Laws of Logic

We are here expounding a distinctly Christian conception of the three laws of logic. These laws of logic do not exist in and of themselves, independent of God. Rather, they reflect the character of God. In particular, they reflect his self-consistency. Or we might equally say that they reflect his love for himself. The Father loves the Son. He will never deviate from that love. That love is love for the Logos, who also expresses the rationality of God.

If the laws reflect the character of God, we must rethink them. They are reflections of the mystery of the Trinity. "Snow is white," as a statement, does not exist in an ideal world independent of the coinherence of the persons of the Trinity, and their coinherent knowledge of the truth that snow is white. The principle of identity is therefore to be reinterpreted. It is an identity that consists in contrast, cohering with variation and distribution. "Snow," "white," and the complete statement "snow is white" have variation and distribution. That is why, among other things, we can consider dirty snowballs and refrozen snow. We can contemplate situations in which we might be inclined to say, "This snow is neither white nor nonwhite, but off-white, or perhaps dirty white." Or we might say, "This snow is white, when we go by first impressions. But it is not white, or at least not pure white, when we go by a detailed analysis of color."

PART III

KINDS OF ANALOGY

We consider the role of analogy in syllogistic reasoning, formal deductive reasoning, inductive reasoning, abductive reasoning, predictive reasoning, scientific models, and verbal communication.

8

Analogy in Varied Contexts

LET US CONSIDER how various kinds of reasoning use analogy. First we consider some instances of *deductive* reasoning, that is, reasoning in which the conclusion follows inevitably from the premises.

Analogy in Syllogistic Reasoning

Let us consider syllogistic reasoning. We consider a particular example:

All mammals are animals.
All dogs are mammals.
Therefore, all dogs are animals.

This syllogism has a specific *content*: it talks about dogs, mammals, and animals, and how the truths about these dogs and mammals and animals relate to other truths. Here is a second sample syllogism, with a different kind of content:

All birds are creatures with wings.
All robins are birds.
Therefore, all robins are creatures with wings.

Both of these instances conform to a particular pattern, sometimes called "Barbara":

All Bs are Cs.
All As are Bs.
Therefore all As are Cs.

This pattern of reasoning is the common *form* belonging to all the particular syllogisms that exhibit the same pattern, the pattern of Barbara. (There are also other syllogistic forms, such as Celarent:

No Bs are As.
All Cs are Bs.
Therefore no Cs are As.)

Let us return to the pattern of Barbara. What is the relation between the particular case with dogs and mammals and the general pattern with As and Bs? The particular case is an instance within the class of all syllogisms that follow the pattern of Barbara. This relation between an instance and a class is the kind of thing that we considered in chapter 6. For the classification to work, we have to understand an analogy between one case and another case, and between each case and the general class. It is easy to see the commonality in this case. The commonality is a commonality of *form*. Each distinct case that conforms to the pattern fills in the form using distinct content. The common form is the general pattern: All Bs are Cs; all As are Bs; therefore all As are Cs. The case above involving dogs, mammals, and animals fills this form with distinct content.

Analogy is present in two additional ways that are more subtle.

One analogy involved in the analysis of a syllogism is a kind of close analogy between form and content. The general form of the syllogism with the pattern "Barbara," with the As and Bs, is not only a form but a form that is supposed to guarantee deductive validity. And deductive validity is an issue concerning *content*. How do we know, just because we have clauses with fixed grammar form, that such constancy of form guarantees that the conclusion, in its content, follows from the premises, in their content?

We actually have to have a kind of insight. The form is not bare form, but at a very general level guarantees a particular logical relationship, a content relationship between the terms. We can be confident about this guarantee only if we can assure ourselves that there is a genuine analogy of a tight kind between form and content. The form and content are not unrelated. The form—at least in a certain respect—reveals something about the content, in its logical relations. In other words, there is an analogy between form and content. In the case of the syllogistic form Barbara, the general form is the pattern: All Bs are Cs; all As are Bs; therefore all As are Cs. This form is analogous to the logical relations that obtain between the As, the Bs, and the Cs within the real world. Or consider a particular case, such as "All mammals are animals; all dogs are mammals; therefore, all dogs are animals." This series of linguistic expressions is a "form." The *content* has to do with logical relations between three propositions about the nature of the world, and the relations of dogs to mammals and to animals.

A second analogy is at work when we consider the relation of propositions in a syllogism—propositions like "all mammals are animals"—to the real world. As we saw earlier, in ordinary language, terms have contrast, variation, and distribution. The variation includes fuzzy boundaries. But a syllogism will fail to be valid if there is an equivocation in one of the terms. For a full guarantee of validity, the terms have to be "pure." That is to say, the terms have to mean exactly the same thing in each of their occurrences. And the boundaries of meaning have to be precise. Typically, when ordinary language is used with respect to the real world, in ordinary personal communicative contexts, the terms are not necessarily "pure." So we have to examine whether the formal argument with the syllogism is analogous in the right way to what the clauses mean when used in a real-world context. This context includes contrast, variation, and distribution in the key terms.[1] For example, depending on the context, the word *dog* could

---

1   Vern S. Poythress, *Logic: A God-Centered Approach to the Foundation of Western Thought* (Wheaton, IL: Crossway, 2013), ch. 19.

denote only domestic dogs (*Canis familiaris*) or could include African wild dogs (*Lycaon pictus*).

Analogy in Other Kinds of Formal Deductive Reasoning

We can also consider other kinds of formal deductive reasoning.[2] First consider the case of a formal language. In the field of logic, a formal language consists of a list of special symbols with rules for combining the symbols. There are no ordinary words. So the system in one sense "has no meaning."[3] Is there no use of analogy either? There is a minimal use of analogy in dealing with the "syntax," that is, the rules for combining symbols. Each well-formed formula is an *instance*, a particular case conforming to the rules. We have to be able to observe that it is analogous to other instances of such well-formed formulas. We are dealing again with the process of classification.

Because the rules are themselves formalized, it may seem easy to test conformity with the rules. But even in the simplest test, we need as human beings to understand the idea of an instance of rule-keeping. In the case of completely formal rules, we can program a computer so that it accurately sorts well-formed formulas from ill-formed sequences of symbols. But someone has to understand the computer code, and to make a judgment as to whether the computer code accomplishes the intended purpose. There is still human involvement at the beginning. And this involvement depends on analogy. There are analogies between distinct pieces of code that are similar in some way. And there is a larger structural analogy between the code and its symbols on the one hand and the conceptual understanding of the purpose of the code on the other hand.

---

2   Note that "deduction" as a term can be used more narrowly (such as deduction in a syllogism or in a proof in geometry) or more broadly (such as in predictions of movements of bodies in space) (Stephen Toulmin, *The Uses of Argument* [Cambridge: Cambridge University Press, 1958], esp. ch. 4).

3   Vern S. Poythress, "Semiotic Analysis of Symbolic Logic Using Tagmemic Theory: With Implications for Analytic Philosophy," *Semiotica*, 2021, https://doi.org/10.1515/sem -2020-0018, https://frame-poythress.org/a-semiotic-analysis-of-symbolic-logic-using -tagmemic-theory-with-implications-for-analytic-philosophy/.

Consider another example, from elementary arithmetic. Arithmetic has a "code" in the form of special symbols such as the numerals "1," "2," and "3," and special signs like "+" and "=." These symbols can be treated merely as symbols. We can perform calculations without paying attention to the meaning of the symbols. But we also have the option of paying attention to the meanings, which apply to bags of apples or oranges or other objects in the real world. We then are using the fact that there is a structural analogy between the symbols on paper and the meanings in the world, meanings about quantities of apples or oranges.

While a specialized formal language is being treated as *merely* formal, there is "no meaning" in a sense. But the long-range goal is typically to use the formal language to represent some kind of deductive reasoning. When we come to look at the representation as a representation of reasoning, we find the same kinds of use of analogy as in the case of syllogisms. The syllogisms in their pure form are analogous to reasonings in language about the world, a world where boundaries are fuzzy. The same need for analogy arises with any deductive system that we eventually employ with respect to reasoning about the real world.

Inductive Reasoning

Next, let us consider inductive reasoning. Inductive reasoning is reasoning that proceeds from individual instances to a general conclusion. One classic case is reasoning about swans. Swan #1 is white. Swan #2 is white. Swan #3 is white. . . . Swan #900 is white. Therefore, all swans are white. (See fig. 8.1.)

Figure 8.1: Inductive Reasoning about Swans

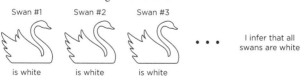

Unfortunately, black swans do exist. They are quite rare, but they exist. Students of reasoning have long recognized that inductive reasoning cannot be made airtight. A mere multiplication of the number of test cases does not guarantee that sometime, somewhere, we will not stumble onto a case that is a rare exception.

Nevertheless, inductive reasoning is useful. We generally rely on well-tested scientific theories, even though they rely on an element of inductive reasoning. Scientists do experiments. They repeat the experiments to see if they come out with the same result. They cannot repeat the experiments an infinite number of times. Nor can they guarantee that they have foreseen what can happen outside the narrow confines of their laboratory. But after awhile, when a theory becomes well established, people cease to worry in practice about the *theoretical* possibility of an exception.

Does inductive reasoning rely on analogy? It does. Each instance that is supposed to test or validate a theory is an instance belonging to the class of all such instances. We have to be able to see an analogy between each of the cases that provide an experimental test. Moreover, we do not want the result to appear consistently only because of some unaccountable detail about the test site. One test site may be located near the sea, at a low elevation. Another test site may be located at a higher location, several thousand feet above sea level. If the test results are consistent at the low elevation, it does not guarantee that nothing will go wrong at the high elevation. Unless we are testing something that is affected by air pressure, we *expect* that the altitude will not make a difference. We think that the cases are analogous in the appropriate way. But if testing reveals otherwise, we know we have to track down why, and maybe have to abandon the claim that our result is universal.

This scenario illustrates the fact that we have to judge not only whether two detailed configurations of experimental apparatus are analogous, but also whether the surrounding circumstances are analogous.

What is the point of observing the presence of analogies? All the analogies go back to God and depend on God. Human reasoning is always imitative of God. God is the source for the analogies. He knows them all completely. And God is the source in a particular *way*, as we have seen. Analogies trace back to the trinitarian character of God.

Abductive Reasoning

Next we consider *abductive* reasoning. Abductive reasoning is usually defined as an inference to the best explanation. Suppose that we consider a crime scene. The detective reasons backward from the evidence to the crime that produced the evidence. This type of reasoning utilizes much knowledge of human nature and of natural causes.

Let us begin with an example of a natural cause. If there is blood on the carpet, and if there is a wound in the dead body, most likely the blood came from the wound. Or did it come from someone in the room weeks ago, who cut his finger? Alternate explanations are always possible, but are they plausible? Are they likely? What is called "the best explanation" is usually not the *only* possible explanation in theory. The detective is tacitly using analogies with other instances of blood flowing and blood staining.

A detective has to deal with human motivations and human causes as well. If anything, this reckoning is even more complex than with many instances of physical causes. Human motivations are often complex. But, by analogy with many other cases, the detective knows that desire for money may be one cause of a crime. Or desire for vengeance. Or pure hatred.

Each crime is unique. But if it were unique in every respect, it would be impossible to make inferences. No crime is an exact repetition of the same crime from an earlier time. But we can see analogies. The detective has to judge whether some analogies are stronger than others, given the evidence. On an elementary level, we differentiate between crimes depending on what laws have been broken. Is it a murder, a theft, a sex crime, a defamation, a lie under oath? Is this crime more likely a crime of passion or a crime of greed?

The rough classification into types of crime also leads us back to our earlier observations about classification. We classify one crime as belonging to a larger class, on account of analogies between the one crime and other crimes belonging to a particular class.

Predictive Reasoning

Inference to the best explanation usually means reasoning backward from effects to their causes. But people can also reason forward from the causes to the effects. They do *predictive* reasoning. In cases of established sciences, we have predictions for the motions of the planets or the motions of rocket ships or projectiles. Less reliably, we have weather predictions. In these cases there are detailed mathematical models, so that there is an analogy of a solid kind between the model and the events in the world that it models. But we can also consider more difficult cases.

Can one predict human history? The trouble is that too many individuals, including prominent individuals like politicians or generals, have a decided influence in the short run, and individuals remain in many respects unpredictable. Yet even in this case, we can try to make tentative predictions based on what we know about particular individuals. In such a case we are using an analogy between the person and what we think we know about the person. We are also, more broadly, in our knowledge of the person, using analogies with many other people that we have known or read about. We understand something about human motivations and personality types and so on.

Scientific Models

Scientific models are closely related to inductive, abductive, and predictive reasoning. At the heart of most scientific models is an analogy between the model itself and the physical processes being modeled. The model may be mathematical or physical or both. The scientists understand that the model is not the reality. But in the case of a well-designed model, it maps the reality. That mapping is a relation of analogy.

The mapping typically allows both predictive reasoning, given a starting state, and reasoning backwards in time to an earlier state of the system. The models in some cases, such as the physics of elementary particles or the general theory of relativity, may be mathematically accurate to several decimal places. In other cases, such as models for weather, the users of the models understand that the models have important limitations. The data about current weather may not be as thorough or as accurate as desired. And the weather model takes into account a large number of influences on weather, but still not everything. Weather is not a closed, isolated system in the way that physical systems can be isolated for some experiments in physics and chemistry.

All in all, many kinds of reasoning use analogies as a crucial element in moving to conclusions.

9

Analogy in Varied Communication

WE MAY CONSIDER how analogy functions in a flexible variety of kinds of communication.

Metaphor as a Form of Analogy

Metaphors are one kind of communication that uses analogy. Isaiah 1:7 says, "foreigners devour your land." In this verse, "devour" is a metaphor. The parallel poetic line says, "It [the land] is desolate, as overthrown by foreigners." The point of the metaphor is that the actions of the foreigners in making the land desolate are to be compared metaphorically to the actions of someone eating food. The eater consumes the food so that little or nothing is left. The plate is empty at the end. By analogy, the land is empty of provisions at the end. It is desolate at the end.

Metaphors use analogies. Max Black[1] in his study of metaphor describes the operation of metaphors as involving a "principal subject" and a "subsidiary subject." The principal subject is the topic that the speaker intends to address principally. In this case, in Isaiah 1:7, it is the topic of the land of Israel, and in the wings are the issues of how the desolation of the land implies a desolation of the people themselves.

---

1 Max Black, *Models and Metaphors: Studies in Language and Philosophy* (Ithaca, NY: Cornell University Press, 1962).

The subsidiary subject is the area of meaning that is used in order to say something insightful about the principal subject. In the case of "devouring" the land, the subsidiary subject is eating.

Max Black observes that a metaphor works by evoking an interaction between the principal subject and the subsidiary subject. The metaphor invites us to compare the two subject areas and to observe ways in which they are alike. With land and food, there is a process of consumption that leads to emptiness or lack of value in what is left. When we are dealing with the two arenas of land and food, the processes of consumption in the two cases are similar but are also obviously different, because they operate in different ways. Different things are consumed, and the consumption is itself different. We have an analogy.

Are we here discussing an instance of reasoning? If we are trying self-consciously to figure out the meaning of Isaiah 1:7, we may find it useful to lay out our thoughts in an explicit way. In that case, we are reasoning about the meaning. Often, however, when we meet a familiar metaphor within our own native language and culture, we do not have to do our reasoning explicitly. We know the meaning immediately, we might say. Nevertheless, even when the result is immediate, this kind of processing of language involves a kind of reasoning underneath the surface. It seems that we are doing something analogous to explicit reasoning. But it happens so fast that we do not slow down to analyze it.

Analogy in Similes

A simile is similar to a metaphor, but the likeness between two subjects is made explicit in language. Consider Isaiah 1:8:

> And the daughter of Zion is left
>> like a booth in a vineyard,
> like a lodge in a cucumber field,
>> like a besieged city.

The three occurrences of the word *like* mark three distinct similes, which are lined up in parallel. Each involves an analogy between the principal subject, the daughter of Zion, and a subsidiary subject. The subsidiary subjects are respectively a booth in a vineyard, a lodge in a cucumber field, and a besieged city. The phrase "daughter of Zion" is itself also a metaphor for the people of Israel, preeminently the people of Jerusalem, which is located on Mount Zion. In each case, both in metaphor and in simile, the wording invites us to explore an analogy between two subject areas.

Antithetical Parallels with Analogy

The extreme case in poetic figures of speech might seem to be the case of antithetical parallels, in which two poetic lines are opposites or antitheses. Here is one case:

> The memory of the righteous is a blessing,
>   but the name of the wicked will rot. (Prov. 10:7)

Even this extreme case involves analogy. Both poetic lines share the broad topic of human moral action (righteous or wicked), the consequences of human action, the reaction of other people who remember, and the theme of blessing or curse. Within this broad framework, the two lines operate as two poles. The differences are differences in the form of opposites. And the theme of opposites is again a theme that unifies the two lines and is therefore also a similarity between the two. We can plot out the similarities and differences in two dimensions, using a table. (See table 9.1.)

Table 9.1: The Memory of the Righteous and the Wicked

	Moral evaluation	Memory	Result
positive pole	righteous	remembered	blessing
antithetical, negative pole	wicked	not remembered or abhorred	curse ("rot")

The column headings organize the similarities, while the two rows organize the contrastive poles. *Within* one column, like the column labeled "moral evaluation," the two rows show the contrasting differences between the two antithetical lines of the proverb.

Analogy in Linguistics

It is also worth observing that processing communication in language constantly relies on analogies between distinct items in language, whether words or phrases or grammatical forms. We have already seen a form of linguistic analogy in dealing with syllogisms. Two syllogisms with the pattern "Barbara" show distinct content but similar form. We have to see that two clauses, such as "All mammals are animals" and "All dogs and mammals," have analogous grammar in order to process them. We could say that the two clauses have the same grammar but distinct content. The two clauses are in this way analogous. People who have learned a language do the grammatical processing so quickly that they do not consciously realize that they are relying on analogy.

We may further illustrate. What is the difference between the two following sequences?

This dog is brown.
is brown dog this.

The first makes grammatical sense, because its structure is analogous to other clauses of the same type. The second does not make grammatical sense. Even here, however, with a broken sequence of words, we as human communicators may try in some circumstances to patch up the breaks. Maybe the person we are listening to has a form of aphasia. He has an idea in his mind about a brown dog, but when he tries to communicate it, it gets broken. We may try to patch it up by unconsciously rearranging the pieces in our mind, until we can construct a clause that has acceptable grammar. So we end up with the first line as our unconscious "correction" of the deviant piece of communication in the second line. In a case like this, we have to rely on an analogy between the deviant order and the normal order. The similarity between the two lies in the shared words. The difference lies in their order (or disorder).

When children learn language, they rely on analogy. Because they overextrapolate, they make mistakes. For example, a child learning English sees that plural nouns in English are made by adding what the linguists might call a pluralizing morpheme -*es*. In spelling, it has the form -*s* or -*es*, depending on the preceding sounds. The child learns that the plural of *dog* is *dogs*, and the plural of *bird* is *birds*. So then he talks about his plural "foots" (for *feet*), and he makes the plural of *mouse* to be *mouses*. His mistakes illustrate that there is a regular pattern in English, and that many plurals are formed in a manner analogous to the formation of other plurals. The exceptions to the pattern make us consciously aware that there *is* a pattern.

What if, in English, each plural had no relation to the singular form? Without some kind of pattern of analogy, it would be tremendously tedious to learn a plural for each noun. Analogy comes to the aid of the child. But the cases of broken analogy make us realize that there is no magic formula that *requires* the plurals to have the same form every time. We have an analogy, not a pure identity.

What is true concerning grammar is also true when we come to sound, to spelling, and to meaning (content). As children learn language, they learn the meanings of words and larger linguistic groupings using analogy. We tend to forget this element of language learning when we are adult native speakers. Meanings come into our mind and language processing happens so fast that it is as if by magic. But analogy has to be there in the background. As a consequence, analogy pervades the functioning of language.

Reasoning in Analogies

In this chapter, we have surveyed a number of kinds of analogies that commonly occur in communication. Are these examples of *reasoning*? Or are they something else? Are they simply observations, rather than reasoning that moves *from* some items of interest to *others*?

Of course the answer depends on how expansive is our idea of *reasoning*. Use of a scientific model or instances of inductive reasoning are more comfortably called "reasoning" because we can see a rational grounding and because they move from some starting point to a conclusion. We move from the model to an application of the model in a particular experimental situation. We move from instances of white swans to a generalization about swans.

The case of linguistic analogy is more challenging. Usually the native speaker does not engage in a self-conscious, laborious process of going from one piece of data to another. From the standpoint of consciousness, it is instantaneous. Or we might say that the important work is done at a subconscious level.

Note that an adult learning a second language may indeed engage in a reasoning process in trying to discern the meaning of a new sentence. Let us suppose that he has been taught some pieces of grammar. He then reasons that the sentence before him is an instance of the grammar he has already learned. Or maybe it is not, but he makes a guess at meaning, based on the larger context. And eventually this guess is either confirmed or disconfirmed, and he learns something more about how the language functions.

The difficulty is that this kind of conscious reasoning by an adult learner is not normal for native speakers. The labor of conscious processing is conspicuous. Similar observations hold for linguists who are analyzing a language. They will often produce a conscious process of reasoning, using a theoretical apparatus. By contrast, for native speakers the process is unconscious. But is subconscious "reasoning" still reasoning? Maybe, but maybe not.

We might postulate, for example, that repeated exposure to instances of language results in some kind of permanent change in the brain, such that the circuits in the brain replace a conscious process of reasoning. What happens when a native speaker reaches this point in his brain wiring? Is the native speaker's reaction then similar to the reaction of an amoeba to a piece of food? The amoeba reacts by moving toward the food and ingesting it. The amoeba is built that way. It does not have to have a conscious reasoning process. It just does what it does.

But we could also postulate a model of the human mind in which there are reasoning processes below the surface of consciousness.

Human beings are still reasoning, but they are not consciously aware of just what they are doing and how they are doing it.

It is probably fruitless at the present state of knowledge to try to match unconscious human powers with the label "reasoning" or "not-reasoning." What we can say is that human beings are *dependent* on the use of linguistic analogies. Without them, we would be helpless in dealing with the English pluralizing morpheme -*s*/-*es*. We may not be able to identify a specific, linear process, consisting in observation and comparison, where the comparison stage invokes specific information that is analogous to the observation. We may not be able to plot out further stages, such as a decision ("yes, this word [*dogs*] is marked as plural"), and an interpretation ("the speaker is talking about more than one dog"). But when we stand back from our immersion in language and begin to analyze, we can see a pattern that shows some kinship with conscious reasoning.

Reasoning in Metaphors

Similar observations extend to the use of metaphors. In ordinary discourse we do not so much consciously analyze metaphors as enjoy them. But an analyst can always come along afterwards and try to explain how we come to enjoy them. And if we meet an unfamiliar metaphor, or a simile like "a lodge in a cucumber field," our reasoning processes may have to become explicit in order to work out the meaning. We ask ourselves in what respect "the daughter of Zion" is like a lodge in a cucumber field. We assemble what we know about the daughter of Zion, and what we know about lodges and cucumber fields, and try to do the best we can to discern what might be the main similarities. Max Black's theory of metaphor, cited above, suggests a process of comparison between the principal subject and the subsidiary subject. The process may be too quick to observe ("instantaneous"). Or it may be difficult to bring the process to the level in which we are fully conscious of what is happening. But however it takes place, we can see a similarity between the unconscious or intuitive interpretation of a metaphor on the one hand, and the later analytic reasoning about the meaning of the metaphor on the other hand.

There are two sides to our observations. On the one side, we run the danger of making the ordinary interpretation of metaphors and linguistic analogies into pieces of self-conscious reasoning, which they are not. On the other side, we run the danger of not acknowledging a considerable degree of similarity between what takes place unconsciously in language use and what takes place self-consciously in later analytic reasoning about that use. So the broader uses of analogy discussed in this chapter are both like and unlike pieces of self-conscious reasoning.

Though the use of analogy is not self-conscious, yet the reliance on analogy is real. And the movement from observation to detection of analogy is rationally justified, even if we cannot capture it as an explicit temporal sequence in consciousness.

10

Tight Analogy and Loose Analogy

WHEN WE LOOK OVER the various kinds of analogy from the previous chapters, we may sense that there is a spectrum. On one end of the spectrum are what might be called "tight" analogies. A tight analogy offers a kind of guarantee for reasoning. At the other end of the spectrum are loose analogies. A loose analogy offers a way to call our attention to some similarity or other, but the similarity involved is "loose" and offers no firm guarantee that we can deduce further consequences.

The Tight End of the Spectrum

The tightest of all analogies is the kind of analogy involved in formal deductive logic. Syllogistic logic is one example. Earlier we considered the example in which all mammals are animals, all dogs are mammals, and therefore all dogs are animals. This is a piece of reasoning in ordinary language, using words like *dogs*.

Any piece of reasoning in ordinary language that matches syllogistic reasoning is a piece of valid reasoning. The match between the standard syllogistic form and the sample piece of reasoning is a "tight" analogy. It seems to guarantee the status of one piece of reasoning (such as the reasoning about dogs). As we have seen, the guarantee is not absolute, because of the possibility of equivocation in the use of a key term. To avoid equivocation, the propositions of a syllogism have to be considered as "isolated" from the world. They are idealized propositions. So there is always a qualification. If we confine our use of the word *validity* only to the "best" cases, valid argumentation occurs only in cases that are sufficiently "isolated." Yet in many of the cases that might be produced, the match is a good one. We seem to be on solid ground in our reasoning.

We might consider the classic case in Western history of deductive reasoning, namely deductive reasoning in geometry, codified by Euclid. This example looks at first glance to be a perfect example. But close inspection shows that it rests on an analogy between lines, circles, and other geometric figures in our world of time and space, and the idealized picture of lines and circles and points in Euclid's subworld of reasoning. In Euclid's world, lines are infinitely long and have no width. Points take up no space. Circles have an infinitely precise radius. The "isolation" of Euclid's idealized picture makes possible rigorous deductions. But when we want to apply geometry to the real world, we find within this world lines that are drawn by pencils or pens, lines that are neither infinitely long nor without width.

Tightness in Scientific Models

In science, mathematical models can also involve tight analogies. In complex situations like weather prediction, the models are often based on adjusting specific variables to an enormous amount of data. The data function in a manner partially parallel to inductive reasoning. Let us suppose that a weather station has collected a huge amount of data about temperature, wind, humidity, and air pressure in a particular region, over a period of decades. If the model matches huge amounts of data already, it will probably match the next bit of data, as yet unknown. In the case of weather prediction, the models do not always work successfully. But models can work impressively well when an experimental apparatus can be isolated from physical interference in order to detect some delicate result. We may take, for example, a measurement of a spectral line in the emissions from atoms of one type. The atoms of this one type are physically isolated from other kinds of atoms, in order to avoid detecting light coming from those other atoms.

This type of physical isolation has some similarities with the kind of "logical" isolation in syllogistic reasoning. We make some restrictions about the environment in which we are working, in order to see a pure, uncontaminated result.

Weather prediction, by contrast, is much less elegant. There are aerodynamic laws governing the movement of gases in space. But "weather" is not isolated from the rest of the world—in particular, from the massive influence of the heat of the sun and the effects of water in the oceans. So a model for weather is more like a "brute force" model. The meteorologists put in massive amounts of data, and then, as if by "force," they conform the mathematics as best they can to the data. (In a typical model, there are still basic mathematical equations for fluid dynamics, both in air and in water, but a lot of adjustments take place through the data that comes in.) We might say that the details of the numerical quantities, for air pressure and air movement and temperature here and there in space, are "isolated" in a computer's memory. They are set apart from other calculations being done for other purposes, and put to one, tightly defined, exclusive use: to produce an overall model that matches the data.

Thus, in both cases there is a kind of movement toward isolation. But in the one case, involving isolating atoms, the movement consists in putting together an experimental apparatus that is shielded from extraneous influences. The apparatus isolates selected atoms from stray physical causes. In the other case, in weather prediction, the movement consists in moving the model itself into conformity with the data.

Loose Analogies

By contrast with the tight analogies, there are at the other end of the spectrum of the various kinds of analogies what we have called *loose* analogies. When we have loose analogies, we need to adjust our expectations. We can draw only limited and more tentative conclusions. In just what way is the daughter of Zion like a lodge in a cucumber field (Isa. 1:8)? It is not so easy to say, especially because modern readers are not so familiar with lodges in cucumber fields. How would we write up a detailed report on the daughter of Zion on the basis of this simile? It does not provide us primarily with prosaic, factual detail, but with an evocation of the mood and the atmosphere of the overall situation.

Fortunately, in this particular case we have three analogies, not one. The daughter of Zion is "left/ like a booth in a vineyard,/ like a lodge in a cucumber field,/ like a besieged city." The three analogies help to qualify each other. They are most likely pointing in the same direction or in overlapping directions, namely the idea of being deserted or isolated.

The verses on either side of the key verse Isaiah 1:8 also help. Verse 7 talks about the land being "desolate." Verse 8 has the key word "left," suggesting isolation. Verse 9 talks about "a few survivors." The main point of comparison seems to be that the booth is in a vineyard, not in a town. The lodge is in the cucumber field, not in a city. And a besieged city is a city that the attacking army has isolated from its surroundings. The larger context of Isaiah 1 is a context of judgment. This context reinforces the idea of desolation or isolation or abandonment.

What we are offered here are three poetically evocative pictures. There is no detailed, exact map between the daughter of Zion and the lodge in the cucumber field. But that is all right, if we interpret the language sensitively and do not force it to map what it does not map. The more prosaic words, such as "desolate," "left," and "survivors" are complemented by the vividness of three pictures of isolation. The vividness evokes deeper human response. We have stirred up within us the emotional echoes of living in isolation or living in a besieged city with a sense of hopelessness, such as may arise when a person does not have aid either from the land or from neighbors.

It is not as if this kind of loose analogy is useless. It is still helpful in its own way. It is more evocative of larger human issues than would be the case for a detailed map. The detailed map invites us to focus very much on the details. The looser analogy may, as it were, raise our eyes to the larger issues of human distress, suffering, depression, and loss. Or, in another context, the issues that are being evoked may be the issues of joy or humility or wisdom. We are still dealing with analogies. In part, it is a matter of an analogy between the human experience of a lodge and the human experience of desolation due to war and captivity. Are we engaging in reasoning? The label "reasoning" may as usual be used more narrowly or more expansively. Expansively, yes, there is implicit reasoning in perceiving the relation of analogy between different human experiences.

If God had wanted for us only to focus all the time on the details, he could have written that way. So we may take the hint and decide that analogies on both ends of the spectrum have their uses.

In the modern West, science has most of the prestige. Poets still exist, but fewer people pay attention to them. For this reason, we need to acknowledge that there is strong cultural pressure to think that scientific reasoning, reasoning using models and tight deductions, is the most powerful and the most important. But human beings cannot cope with life without dealing with larger meanings. Poetry is not in fact dead. In the broad sense of "poetry," influential poetry or at least artistic expression comes to us in our popular songs and movies.

So the loose analogies that occur in metaphors and in other figures of speech, as well as in visual symbols, still play a role in modern cultures. They have a role in the Bible as well, as illustrated by Isaiah 1:8 and other poetic passages. They can communicate truth and also evoke deep human responses.

PART IV

GUIDANCE FOR ANALOGY

*We look at principles for guiding the wise use
of analogy, especially the use of context.*

11

Guidance in the Use of Analogy

ANALOGIES COME in a great variety. So what guides our sense of how far an analogy "works"? How do we know, for example, when a syllogism is actually valid and when it fails because of equivocation? How do we know when a scientific model is likely to succeed and when it is likely to fail? How do we know what claim is being made when the daughter of Zion is compared to a lodge in a cucumber field? Good reasoning includes wisdom in the appropriate assessment of analogies.

The Key Role of Context

Do we simply take cases involving analogy one by one? And if we do, does that imply that there is no general rule?

In all the disparate cases, context has a role. Depending on the case, the key guidance may come from one or more components of the context. The context is always there as an influence.

So, for example, with syllogistic reasoning, we do have to see whether a syllogism involving claims about the real world has an equivocation. In order to judge equivocation, we look at meanings in relation to the world being described.

With a scientific model, it depends on what kind of model we are using. Is the model a model that is supposed to work best for some physically isolated experimental apparatus (e.g., a device for measuring a spectral emission line of some atom)? Then the appropriate context to inspect is the context of physical isolation or lack of it.

Or is the model intended to work because it has massive data supplied from a real-world situation, as is the case with weather models? Then we have to look at whether the data are accurate, whether key data points are missing (no data available from some geographical locations or some altitudes), and whether the conditions are exceptional (as with a hurricane or a tsunami). Exceptional conditions are not necessarily a barrier. It depends on whether the model is designed to deal with the exceptions as well as with "typical" weather.

With a one-time metaphor, such as in Isaiah 1:8, we have to look especially at the literary context. What do neighboring verses suggest might be the main points? And does our knowledge of the external world give us some ideas about what is common to a booth in a vineyard, a lodge in a cucumber field, and a besieged city?

Extended Contexts

With each use of analogy comes a context. But in fact, the ultimate context for Isaiah 1:8 or for a model for weather prediction is the context of the whole world. Context extends out indefinitely, in multiple directions. The context for weather in Philadelphia is first of all the information about wind and temperature and humidity in the immediate vicinity of Philadelphia. But then our circle of context might move out to the Atlantic seaboard in one direction and the interior of the country in the other direction. And it might move out to measure more factors, such as sunshine, pollution, and variations in temperature and pressure at different heights in the atmosphere.

We must have some sense, often intuitive, as to what is *relevant* within a context that extends outward indefinitely. This sense of relevance itself depends on using analogies.

For example, the context of one scientific experimental setup evokes the larger pattern of *all* such experimental setups within a particular subdiscipline (let us say spectroscopy). And this subdiscipline evokes a larger context of disciplined understanding about the general outlines of how procedures for physical isolation function across a whole host of subdisciplines. People trained in science have absorbed tacitly a complex understanding of how experimental science "works." So, when they look at a single experiment, they know it is analogous to other experiments. They rely on analogy with these other experiments. They rely also on analogy with the experiences of scientists trying to track down causes of interference in other experiments. They know that they have to look for what has been put in place in the present experiment, in order to head off interference from unwanted causes.

Because of the focus on the experimental apparatus itself, as the source of key results, it is easy to ignore the role of the environment in which there are procedures of isolation. It is easy also to ignore the role of analogy, analogy holding with a multitude of other cases in science, because this analogy mostly remains tacit, not explicit. But it has to be there. Michael Polanyi makes a point about the role of context in writing about the personal involvement of the scientist and the role of tacit understanding.[1] Scientific results can at times have a most impressive rigor as well as yielding impressive insights. But the rigor and the insights come in a way guided by a host of analogies with the larger framework of science.[2]

---

1   Michael Polanyi, *Personal Knowledge: Towards a Post-Critical Philosophy* (Chicago: University of Chicago Press, 1964); Michael Polanyi, *The Tacit Dimension* (Garden City, NY: Anchor Books, 1967).

2   Relevant at this point is the work of Thomas S. Kuhn, *The Structure of Scientific Revolutions* (Chicago: University of Chicago Press, 1970), with his idea of the influence of a disciplinary matrix or framework ("paradigm") within a particular field of science.

12

Context in God

TO UNDERSTAND MORE DEEPLY the role of analogy, we need to return to the archetype for analogy, which is in God.

Looking Again at the Archetype

As we saw earlier, even apart from the creation of the world or Christ's role in redemption, the Son is the eternal image of God (Col. 1:15), "the exact imprint of his nature" (Heb. 1:3). The archetypal analogy is the analogy between the Father and the Son. The analogy combines similarity (common nature) and difference (the distinction of persons).

The Holy Spirit in Context

What is the role of the Holy Spirit? The Holy Spirit is one with the Father and the Son. The Holy Spirit offers the archetypal context for the love between the Father and the Son. The Holy Spirit "searches everything, even the depths of God" (1 Cor. 2:10). This searching naturally includes a comprehensive knowledge of the one divine nature, which belongs to "the depths of God." But does it not naturally *also* include a comprehensive knowledge of the *relation* between the Father and the Son? If the Holy Spirit knows "everything," as the verse says, his knowledge includes knowledge of the person of the Father, and the person of the Son, and the distinction between the Father and the Son, and comprehensive knowledge of the relation of *imaging*, of the texture of the Son being "the exact imprint." (See fig. 12.1.)

Figure 12.1: Context for the Archetypal Image of God

Thus the Trinity, and the three persons in their distinctions from each other, offer the archetype for all three aspects of analogy, as we have explored them in previous chapters. God, especially in the person of the Father, is the archetype for similarities found in the analogies that we use. God the Son is preeminently the archetype for the differences found in an analogy. God the Spirit is preeminently the archetype for the context, which guides and qualifies the nature of the analogy.

The three persons of the Trinity indwell each other. They coinhere. Consequently, they are inseparable. By analogy, similarities, differences, and contexts are inseparable in the derivative, ectypal instances of analogy that we explore in human reasoning. (See fig. 12.2.)

The context in God is infinitely deep. As an example, consider the Father's knowledge of the Son, mentioned in Matthew 11:27. The Father knows the Son. And, by coinherence, the Father dwells in the Son. So in knowing the Son, the Father knows also the Father dwelling in the Son. He knows the Spirit dwelling in the Son. The Father knows these things by indwelling the Son's knowledge of the Father. He knows comprehensively how the Spirit searches the depths of God. He knows also the Spirit's knowledge of the Son's being the exact imprint of the divine nature.

Figure 12.2: The Trinitarian Archetype for Analogies in Human Reasoning

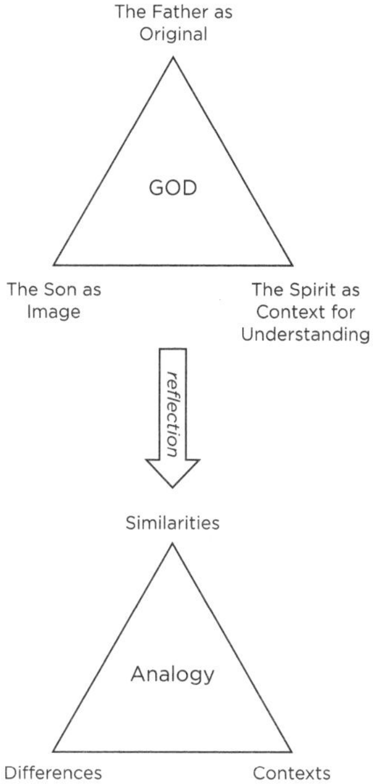

This archetypal pattern, in which contexts are embedded in contexts, is mirrored or reflected in human analogical reasoning. Isaiah 1:8 has an immediate literary context. And that context of a few verses has the larger context of the whole first chapter of Isaiah, and that context in turn is embedded in the whole book of Isaiah. But there are also smaller and larger contexts out in the world: the "daughter of Zion" focuses first of all on the people inhabiting Mount Zion. But that group of people stands for the whole southern kingdom, and the southern kingdom stands for the whole people of God constituted by the southern and northern kingdoms together. And through Abram "all the families of the earth shall be blessed" (Gen. 12:3). Abraham's descendants exist in a context in which God's plan aims to include other nations. And then there is the context of cucumbers and cucumber fields and analogies between various aspects of the created order.

A Perspective on an Analogy

We can see how the Holy Spirit offers an archetype for context in another way. When we consider an analogy, it is an analogy between two things, two distinct subject-matters. To study an analogy is to focus partly on the *relation* between two subject-matters. And, as above, the Holy Spirit is the archetype for *relations* in the Trinity.

The archetypal analogy is the analogy between the Father and the Son, as expressed in Hebrews 1:3, "the exact imprint of his nature." To see the analogy properly, the viewer has to have in mind both the Father and the Son and the relation between the two.

Now consider the human level, and focus on an analogy between two human beings. Adam fathered a son, Seth, after his image (Gen. 5:3). To consider the analogy between Adam and Seth, we position ourselves as a third human being, who is distinct from them both. The archetype for this "positioning" is found in God, in the Holy Spirit who is distinct from the Father and the Son. (See fig. 12.3.)

Figure 12.3: The Spirit Knowing the Relation of the Father and the Son

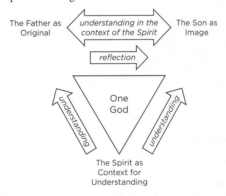

But someone may ask whether Adam himself can appreciate the analogy between himself and his son Seth. The answer is that he can. He can because he can "stand back" from his experience of immersion in a relation to his son, and can take a kind of birds-eye view of both himself and his son. Perhaps he compares the Adam-

Seth relation to the Seth-Enosh relation (Gen. 4:26). This kind of standing-back is an instance of mini-transcendence. We temporarily use a perspective in which we rise above the immediacy of the circumstances. These perspectives imitate God, who is unique in his omniscience. He knows all perspectives and is the archetypal case of a personal being who is able to "stand back" and take in a whole scene—even the whole of history. So Adam's act of thinking about his relation to Seth still presupposes God and his ability to have personal perspectives.

The Archetype for Tight Analogies

In the case of tight analogies, the similarities between the two poles of the analogy are impressively stable. The archetype for this strong similarity is found in the *perfect* case of similarity in God. The Son is "the exact imprint of his nature" (Heb. 1:3). The match between the Father and the Son is "exact"; it is perfect. The Father is God; the Son is God. The two persons are exactly the same God. The Holy Spirit also is the same God. This exact match is the foundation for matches found derivatively, when we look at the created order.

In the case of some scientific models, the match is mathematically exact. Some predictions in quantum field theory are confirmed to ten parts in a billion or better. This degree of "exactness" in a match is due to God's control of the providential order. So its archetype must be found in exactness of match in the persons of the Trinity.

The Archetype for Loose Analogies

What about loose analogies? In loose analogies, the differences are more visible. What has the daughter of Zion to do with a lodge in a cucumber field? Not so much. Does this kind of analogy have a root in God, and if so, how?

One way of proceeding is to reflect on how differences arise within the created order. God specifies them. He separated the light from the darkness (Gen. 1:4). He separated the waters below from the waters above (v. 7). The distinctions reflect God's word, which specifies them.

And God's word directed to creation reflects God's eternal Word, the second person of the Trinity.

When we are using analogies, we are imitating God. We are imitating him not only in one way but in three ways: with respect to similarities, with respect to differences, and with respect to the context guiding the use of similarities and differences.

13

Perspectives on Ethics,
Applied to Analogies

WE CONTINUE TO consider the question of how we have guidance in our reasoning as we assess the implications of an analogy and also its limitations. What do we need as we assess either the validity of a syllogistic form of reasoning or the use of a simile ("like a lodge in a cucumber field")?

The issue of guidance is a *normative* issue. How do we get *good* guidance? What counts as good reasoning?

The field of ethics is often considered narrowly as a field asking and answering questions about moral right and wrong. Moral right and wrong have to do with the value of various human actions. But if we consider ethics expansively, we can see that it impinges on the question of *norms* for actions, including norms for *reasoning*.

Three Perspectives on Ethics

John Frame introduces three perspectives that function together in ethical decision-making (see ch. 2). They are the normative perspective, the situational perspective, and the existential perspective.[1] These

---

1   John M. Frame, "A Primer on Perspectivalism (Revised 2008)," §7, https://frame-poythress
    .org/a-primer-on-perspectivalism-revised-2008/, accessed April 25, 2020; Vern S.
    Poythress, *Knowing and the Trinity: How Perspectives in Human Knowledge Imitate the
    Trinity* (Phillipsburg, NJ: P&R, 2018), ch. 13.

three perspectives are not independent of one another but interlocking. Properly treated, each reinforces the others. (See fig. 13.1.)

Figure 13.1: Three Perspectives on Ethics

Application to Guidance for Analogies

Now what relevance do these perspectives have when we treat the use of analogies in reasoning? We have seen that there are two kinds of analogies, tight analogies and loose analogies. The tight analogies can be further subdivided, depending on the way in which the tight relation is achieved.

Normatively focused tight analogies. In the case of the scientific model, the model may take the form of a description of fundamental scientific laws, such as the laws of chemistry. The laws function like norms. But to see the laws confirmed by experiment, the experimental apparatus has to be protected from interference. In other words, it has to be protected from a larger *situation*. It has to be isolated from normal complexities with situations. Let us call this kind of analogy a *normative-focused* analogy.

In fact, the use of a model depends on the interaction of normative, situational, and existential perspectives. The norms often have the form of major scientific laws. The experimenter has to check the situation to make sure it includes the appropriate isolation. And the experimenter has to be there in person, with his existential contribution, and his ability to evaluate both the relevance of the laws within the apparatus and the achievement of isolation in the situation. All three perspectives are functioning. And yet the normative perspective naturally dominates, because it is the laws and the desire to test or confirm the laws that dictate what happens in the situational and existential perspectives.

Situationally focused tight analogies. A second form of scientific model is typically used in situations like weather prediction. The weather, as we observed, cannot be isolated. So the situation, the data about the weather, dominates the use of the model. The situational perspective is dominant. And yet the normative perspective is also necessary. There is a weather model that is constructed using underlying laws of aerodynamics and heat and temperature. The laws function as norms. Let us call this kind of analogy a *situational-focused* analogy.

Once again, the existential perspective is also in operation. The person engaging in weather prediction makes sure that the right data is fed into the computational model. He has to judge whether there is enough data, what is its quality, and whether it makes it into the model in appropriate form. He also has to judge whether the computational model adequately represents the laws of nature. If the result is counterintuitive, he goes back and rechecks the process.

Thus this kind of case highlights the function of the situational perspective. But if one is careful in analyzing the case, one does not deny the presence of the other two perspectives. The other two perspectives still interlock with the situational perspective. Reasoning by analogy involves the interaction of all three perspectives.

Loose Analogies and Existential Focus

Loose analogies are more closely related to the existential perspective. Let us consider the reasoning that is involved if we try to work out the meaning of Isaiah 1:8, with its language about a lodge in a cucumber field. There is no well-established model that functions as the main articulation of the analogy. The analogy comes up on the spot, so to speak. The spontaneous and unpredictable character of a loose analogy puts a certain premium on the personal recipient. He has to use all kinds of knowledge, without knowing at the beginning which aspects of knowledge may be most pertinent.

The person's abilities are central, and so we may say that the person is central or that the existential perspective has a dominant role. Yet, as usual, the existential perspective does not operate independently of the other two perspectives. There are *norms* guiding the decision as to *which* features are similar and *which* features are different when the personal recipient begins to judge the meaning and implications of the analogy.

Moreover, there is always some form of *situational* context. For example, in Isaiah 1:8, we might ask, "What is happening or threatening to happen to the daughter of Zion? And what is a lodge in a cucumber field actually like?" We might mentally go out and look at the state of things in the world, the state of the situation. Yet, as we observed, the existential perspective has dominance. We may say that a loose analogy in reasoning is also an *existential-focused* analogy. It goes together with other analogies used in reasoning, namely normative-focused tight analogies and situational-focused tight analogies (see fig. 13.2).

Figure 13.2: Three Kinds of Analogies

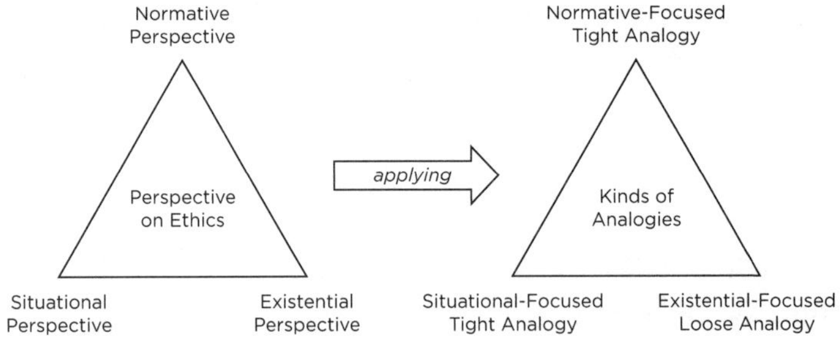

Kinds of Analogies Reflecting the Trinity

John Frame's three perspectives on ethics reflect the Trinitarian character of God, as we observed earlier (ch. 2, esp. table 2.4).[2] The three

---

2   Poythress, *Knowing and the Trinity*, ch. 13.

perspectives on ethics also reflect the three perspectives on Lordship, namely authority, control, and presence. The interlocking of the three perspectives on ethics reflects the "interlocking" of the persons of the Trinity in their coinherence.[3]

Since the three kinds of analogies reflect the three perspectives on ethics, the three kinds also reflect the Trinity. Since any one analogy involves attention to norms, to situation, and to personal acts of judgment, any one analogy reflects the three perspectives on ethics and also then reflects the Trinity. (See fig. 13.3.)

Figure 13.3: The Trinity Reflected in Analogies

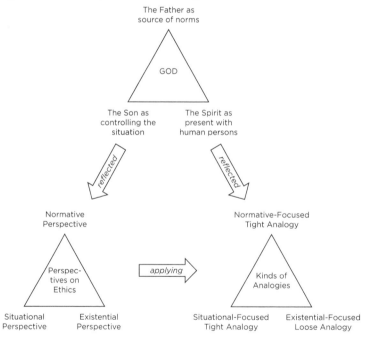

Analogies are innately mysterious. Their mystery is reflective of the mystery of the Trinity. *Reasoning* using an analogy is therefore also mysterious. The mystery cannot be fully dissolved by human analysis.

---

3   Poythress, *Knowing and the Trinity*, 147.

14

Judicial Deliberations

LET US NOW CONSIDER another use of analogy in reasoning, namely in judicial deliberations. We have already considered the use of abductive reasoning in the case of a detective analyzing the scene of a crime (ch. 8). A similar challenge occurs in the case of a trial involving a crime. In a trial, a judge or a jury has to decide whether the defendant is guilty or innocent. Their decision is supposed to be based on whether they think the defendant committed the crime specified in the indictment by the prosecution. This decision is a case of inference to the best explanation (see ch. 8).

Human Ability to Reason about Crime

Human reasoning about a crime is never airtight. Our knowledge is finite. And the evidence presented in court is finite. Yet the trial system expects the judge or a jury to arrive at a reasonable judgment. It will not be an infallible judgment, but it still should be a reasonable judgment. The assumption is that human rationality has capabilities for doing what is reasonable in a complex case that involves analogies.

To judge a case of crime involves many analogies. There are analogies with other crimes, analogies with other kinds of human beings and other instances of human behavior, analogies with other circumstances showing what are the likely causal sequences. When there are witnesses, the judge or jury has to weigh their credibility, as well as to listen to what they say. How can human reasoning bring together all these sources, with their many analogies? Somehow people do it. (See fig. 14.1.)

Figure 14.1: Working with Analogies in Judicial Deliberation

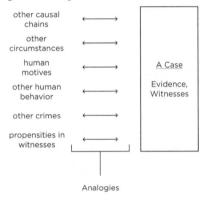

Analogies

Divine Foundation for Judgment

The expectation for reasonable or wise judgment has a divine foundation. In the Old Testament, in the time of Moses, a system for judicial judgment was set up. Moses began by doing it all himself, but then he appointed subordinate judges (Ex. 18). Hard cases were supposed to be sent on to Moses, in a kind of "appeal" process (vv. 22, 26). Moses was the spokesman for God, so it might be the case that he received infallible divine revelations about these cases. But other places in the law of Moses indicate that there is to be a permanent judicial system, which is supposed to continue after Moses is dead (Ex. 23:3; Lev. 19:15; Deut. 16:18–20; 17:8–20). In these instructions we find a stress on impartiality, on not taking a bribe, and on being instructed by the law. All these guidelines come in contexts where the judges themselves are not guaranteed infallibility. The witnesses also are fallible. So two witnesses are required to confirm a matter (Deut. 17:6; 19:15–21).

The record subsequently shows that even the requirement of two witnesses can fail (1 Kings 21:13). Yet this failure, due to human sin, does not invalidate the entire structure of the judicial system. Rather, it is a failure in individual cases. If judges, rather than witnesses, are corrupt, they extend the failure more broadly and deeply. (Think of the injustice from the Sanhedrin and from Pilate when Jesus was sentenced to be crucified.) Yet the principle from God remains true, that he appoints authorities with the task of executing justice on earth (Rom. 13:1–5).

Contextual Skill

The divine principle that human beings can make judicial judgments implies a corresponding ability. We should not conclude that everyone is equally gifted in judging, but at least that judicial judgment is possible in principle, within the limits of humanity. First Corinthians 6:5 affirms variations in judicial skill when it asks, "Can it be that there is no one among you *wise enough* to settle a dispute between the brothers?"

So how does a human being make a judicial judgment, and at least sometimes do it well? When many factors are involved, as in some crime cases, the existential element in human judgment plays an obvious role. Surely the human judge has to take into account analogies based on situations, based on human personality types, based on probable human motivations. But he *also* has to be able to integrate these disparate sources wisely.

When he became king, Solomon was concerned about having the ability to rule the people well. Solomon asked God for *wisdom* (1 Kings 3:5, 9, 12). The subsequent narrative in 1 Kings shows us a hard case (vv. 16–28). The case illustrates the *need* for wisdom. It also confirms that God's promise to give wisdom to Solomon has come true.

Solomon in this respect is a type or shadow of Christ to come (Matt. 12:42). All wisdom is to be found in Christ: "in whom [Christ] are hidden all the treasures of wisdom and knowledge" (Col. 2:3). The integrating skill exercised in the wisdom found in the human mind reflects the wisdom of Christ.

Christ is wise with respect to both his human nature (Luke 2:52) and his divine nature. He is the wisdom of God (1 Cor. 1:30). When we are united to Christ, we "have the mind of Christ" (1 Cor. 2:16).

These verses underline the key role played by the analogy between a human mind filled with the Spirit of Christ and the divine mind found in Christ himself, as the second person of the Trinity.

Bringing Analogies Together

We can see that in this respect, as in others, human reasoning reflects the divine mind. Judicial judgments on earth bring together many disparate analogies touching on many aspects of the situation and the crime. This bringing together has its foundation in the unity of the divine mind. God knows all things. He does not merely know a truth here and a truth there; he knows truth as one whole. All truth holds together in the one mind of God. We bring together analogies in imitation of the divine unity of the divine mind.

Yet at the same time we see difference. We are finite. The bringing together that we do in our minds never encompasses all possible truths. And the process of bringing together, in our human judgments, is a process in time. We consider first one thing, then another. In time, we advance in our reasoning from one inference to another. God, by contrast, knows all things at all times, and is not captive within time. There are no "inferences" for God, if by inference we mean the kind of progress in time that moves from one truth to another previously unknown truth.

At the same time, as we have observed, God's truth and faithfulness and self-consistency are the very foundation for the laws of logic and the processes of inference. In our human reasoning we are reflecting the harmony of God, a harmony in which all truths fit together.

Mystery in Rationality

It follows that, at their best, judicial judgments on earth are rational but also mysterious. The mystery cannot be dissolved by some further insight, because we can never be conscious of all contexts at once and harmonize them all in a single sweep of exhaustive consciousness and exhaustive knowledge.

Judicial judgments reflect the authority that God has given to human authorities (Rom. 13:1–5). In this respect they are among the most exalted of human actions. If these are mysterious, then we cannot hope to model human rationality fully, using as our standard *only* the kind of tightly analogical logic found in syllogisms or modern symbolic logic. Tight logic has its role, as we have repeatedly affirmed. But it is a mistake to think that it is the one essential key to rationality. This limitation belonging to formal logic applies when we attempt to understand human rationality. But it applies all the more for when we attempt to understand divine rationality. Divine rationality, not our tight symbolic logic as such, is the archetype for human rationality.

Divine rationality is mysterious. So human rationality derivatively is mysterious. We see the mystery confirmed when we contemplate what it meant for Solomon to be wise, as set out in 1 Kings 3.

PART V

DERIVING PERSPECTIVES ON RATIONALITY

We consider some important perspectives on rationality.

15

The Idea of a Perspective

IN THE NEXT CHAPTERS we want to explore how several aspects of the use of analogy in reasoning can be seen as related to perspectives, and the perspectives in turn as related to the Trinity. As we shall see, the structure of perspectives informs us about the nature of analogies and the nature of reasoning.

Let us begin with the general idea of a perspective. A perspective is a view of something from somewhere by someone.[1] For example, suppose that Alice is looking at her pet rabbit, who is in her fenced-in yard. Alice has a spatial perspective on her rabbit, from the spatial location where she is standing.[2] The perspective is her view of the rabbit. The "somewhere" is the place where she is standing, which gives her a particular view, facing the rabbit's front or back or left side—whichever it may be. And she herself is the "someone" who is using the perspective.

More precisely, a perspective is an *analogical* view of something from somewhere by someone.[3] In the case of a spatial perspective like Alice's, the analogy is comparatively straightforward. There is an analogy between Alice's two-dimensional visual experience on the one hand and the actual rabbit on the other hand. Not only can we view

---

1   Vern S. Poythress, *Knowing and the Trinity: How Perspectives in Human Knowledge Imitate the Trinity* (Phillipsburg, NJ: P&R, 2018), 11, 262.
2   Poythress, *Knowing and the Trinity*, ch. 2.
3   Poythress, *Knowing and the Trinity*, 262–65.

the rabbit from other locations, but we can consider aspects of the rabbit that are not visual. We could feel the rabbit's fur, or read about its internal organs. The rabbit is more than Alice's two-dimensional visual snapshot; but the visual snapshot does inform us about the real rabbit.

The "somewhere" and the "someone" are key in establishing and using an analogy. So we can grow in our appreciation of analogy by thinking about perspectives.

Source of Perspectives

We earlier used John Frame's three perspectives on ethics: the normative perspective, the situational perspective, and the existential perspective. These three perspectives reflect the structure belonging to the Trinity (ch. 2).[4] Moreover, these three perspectives can be used as a starting point to analyze and understand a single perspective. Let us see how it works.[5]

A perspective is a view of something from somewhere by someone. The view itself functions like a norm for the person who is using a perspective. The view he has of the object guides his understanding concerning what he is analyzing. So, as a first point, the normative perspective is closely related to the view that is used, and then also to the object being viewed.[6]

Second, the situational perspective focuses naturally on the environment in which perspectival thinking is happening. The immediate environment is the "somewhere" used by the perspective. Consider a spatial perspective. Alice looks at her pet rabbit from the spatial position in which she stands. Her spatial position results in a perspective in which some parts of the rabbit are visible and others are not. This spatial position is the "somewhere" aspect of the perspective.

We can also consider thematic perspectives.[7] A thematic perspective is a view of something where we focus on one theme. Alice can consider

---

4 Poythress, *Knowing and the Trinity*, ch. 13.

5 Poythress, *Knowing and the Trinity*, ch. 29.

6 The discussion of perspectives on a perspective in *Knowing and the Trinity*, ch. 29, correlated the normative perspective with the *view* of an object. But the object itself can obviously not be excluded as one kind of guide for a person's knowledge of the object. The object and the view imply each other.

7 Poythress, *Knowing and the Trinity*, ch. 4.

her rabbit with respect to the theme of beauty or the theme of health or the theme of the physical activities of its muscles. A theme functions as a defining focus for the study. But to undertake this kind of study, one must already know something about the theme. There must already be a context, a kind of metaphorical "somewhere" making the theme meaningful when Alice considers her rabbit. Thus, the situational perspective has a close correlation to the "somewhere" aspect in the function of a perspective.

Third, the existential perspective in ethics invites us to focus on the persons and their motives. This focus leads naturally to focusing on the "someone" who is using a perspective. What motives and inclinations guide this person's use of the perspective?

In sum, the three perspectives on ethics correlate with three perspectives on a perspective. The normative, situational, and existential perspectives on ethics correlate respectively with three aspects belonging to a single perspective, namely the aspect of "view of something," the aspect of "somewhere," and the aspect of "someone." We can consider these three aspects of a single perspective as three perspectives *on* a perspective. We can name them respectively the theme-focused perspective, the context-focused perspective, and the person-focused perspective[8] (table 15.1).

Table 15.1: Perspectives on a Perspective

Perspectives on ethics:	Normative perspective	Situational perspective	Existential perspective
Aspects of a perspective:	view of something	from somewhere	by someone
Perspectives on a perspective:	theme-focused perspective	context-focused perspective	person-focused perspective

The pattern of unity, diversity, and interlocking (coinherence) that we find in the triad of perspectives on ethics is reflected in the corresponding triad for perspectives on a perspective. (See fig. 15.1.)

8   Poythress, *Knowing and the Trinity*, 266–68.

Now what is the significance of this pattern for our reasoning? It shows one more way in which the pattern of the Trinity is reflected in our reasoning. This time the pattern occurs in reasoning using a perspective.

Figure 15.1: The Triad for Ethics Reflected in the Triad for Perspectives on a Perspective

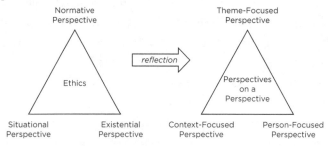

Derivation of Perspectives from the Trinity

Since the persons of the Trinity are reflected in the triad for ethics (fig. 2.2), they are also reflected in the triad for perspectives on a perspective. (See fig. 15.2.)

Figure 15.2: The Trinity Reflected in Perspectives on a Perspective

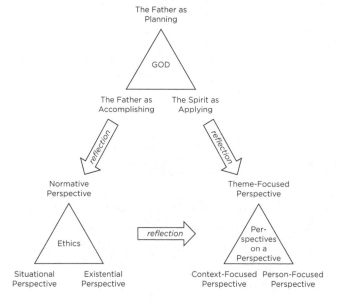

Analogy and Perspectives

What does analogy have to do with using perspectives in reasoning? Analogy is operative when we consider an object of study using a theme. The theme, as indicated above, is used against the background of previous knowledge. So an analogy exists between the previous knowledge and the present object of study. The analogy exists, we might say, in the interface between the view of the object and the "somewhere" informing the view. Or it exists in the interface between a theme-focused perspective and a context-focused perspective.[9]

---

9 The discussion of perspectives on a perspective in Poythress, *Knowing and the Trinity*, ch. 29, places analogy *within* a theme. A theme, when used as a perspective on a subject-matter, has an aspect of analogy built into it. But this analogy works only if there is already a background of understanding of some instances of the theme. So there is a sense in which analogy operates in the relation of background knowledge to the subject-matter in question.

16

Perspectives by Persons of the Trinity

LET US NOW APPLY the idea of perspectives on a perspective to understand what happens with the persons of the Trinity.

Unlimited Knowledge in the Trinity

Each person in the Trinity has unlimited knowledge, because each person is God. So the term *perspective*, if used at all with respect to a person of the Trinity, must be used with this key difference in mind. The use of the term *perspective* is analogical, in that it does not function in completely the same way for man and for God.[1]

Knowledge by the Father

The Bible indicates that each person in the Trinity has *personal* knowledge. According to Matthew 11:27, "no one knows the Son except the Father, and no one knows the Father except the Son and anyone to whom the Son chooses to reveal him." The Father, as the Father, has personal knowledge of the Son. This affirmation has meaning in relation to the idea of a personal perspective.[2] The Father, as a person, has a perspective on the Son. And we can distinguish this perspective from the personal perspective that the Son has on the Father. In both cases

---

1   Vern S. Poythress, *Knowing and the Trinity: How Perspectives in Human Knowledge Imitate the Trinity* (Phillipsburg, NJ: P&R, 2018), 270–71.

2   Poythress, *Knowing and the Trinity*, chs. 3 and 30.

the knowledge is the entire, unlimited knowledge of God. But that is compatible with our affirming the distinction of the persons.[3]

The person of the Father is in focus if we use the *person*-focused perspective on the Father's personal perspective. The Son is in focus if we use the *theme*-focused perspective, because the Son is in a sense the "theme" of the Father's knowledge.[4] The Father's knowledge also takes place in an "environment," the environment of the Holy Spirit as expressive of the love between the Father and the Son (John 3:34–35). Thus the Holy Spirit is in focus if we use the *context*-focused perspective. (See table 16.1.)

Table 16.1: Persons and Perspectives on the Father's Knowledge

God the Father	God the Son	God the Holy Spirit
person-focused perspective	theme-focused perspective	context-focused perspective

In this case, the distinctions among the persons of the Trinity, together with their unity, is the archetypal pattern. The three perspectives are ectypal reflections or derivatives. (See fig. 16.1.)

Figure 16.1: The Trinity Reflected in Personal Perspectives

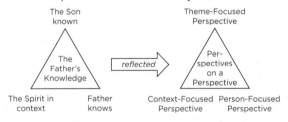

---

3   Vern S. Poythress, *The Mystery of the Trinity: A Trinitarian Approach to the Attributes of God* (Phillipsburg, NJ: P&R, 2020), ch. 47.

4   The theme-focused perspective focuses on the "theme," which is distinguishable from the object on which the person focuses. All knowledge that God has is deeply mysterious. Yet it still makes sense, for both human knowledge and divine knowledge, that knowledge of any one truth exists along with a larger body of truth. The entire knowledge about the Son is like a theme with which to approach any one truth about the Son.

Does this analysis "explain" the structure of the Father's knowledge? No. It is all mysterious. What we are doing is little more than explaining or restating in an alternate form the natural meaning involved in saying that the Father knows the Son. Moreover, we have to affirm the other kinds of personal knowledge within the Trinity: the Son knows the Father, the Father knows the Spirit, the Spirit knows the Father, and so on.

Knowledge by the Son

We may similarly consider the Son's knowledge of the Father. The Son is in focus when we use the person-focused perspective. The Father is in focus when we used the theme-focused perspective. And the Spirit is in focus when we use the context-focused perspective (table 16.2).

Table 16.2: Persons and Perspectives on the Son's Knowledge

God the Son	God the Father	God the Holy Spirit
person-focused perspective	theme-focused perspective	context-focused perspective

Knowledge by the Holy Spirit

We may also consider knowledge by the Holy Spirit, as it is set forth in 1 Corinthians 2:10–11: "For the Spirit searches everything, even the depths of God. For who knows a person's thoughts except the spirit of that person, which is in him? So also no one comprehends the thoughts of God except the Spirit of God."

In these verses the Holy Spirit is the knower. The Holy Spirit is in focus when we use the person-focused perspective. The object of knowledge is "the depths of God," and also "the thoughts of God." These are two descriptions of the same thing, namely everything that God knows. The depths of God are in focus when we use the theme-focused perspective. All three persons know all that God knows. But the Father is preeminently the one who represents God in many instances. So we can also say that the Father is in focus when we use the theme-focused perspective.

What about the context-focused perspective? The context here is the context of the power to search. In this context, the term "search" does not, of course, imply a limitation. We are not supposed to think that the Spirit has to search out within time things that he does not originally know and that he later comes to know. The Spirit always has all the knowledge of God. But the expression about "searching" still indicates that in a mysterious way there is eternal activity in God. In fact, this activity is the eternal archetype for human beings, when they act to search things out, either in a physical search in space or a mental search in mental "space." They do so through the presence of the Holy Spirit (Job 32:8).

Among human beings, searches involve the execution of plans. In these executions, human beings are imitating God. God the Father is the preeminent original planner, and God the Son is the one who preeminently executes the plan of the Father.[5] The archetype of human action is found in divine action. And this divine action is differentiated action, the action of the Father, and of the Son, and of the Holy Spirit. So we may infer that the "execution" of knowledge by the Holy Spirit, as he "searches," is an execution through the presence of the Son. The Son is in focus when we use the context-focused perspective (table 16.3).

Table 16.3: Persons and Perspectives on the Holy Spirit's Knowledge

God the Spirit	God the Father	God the Son
person-focused perspective	theme-focused perspective	context-focused perspective

As is to be expected, the person highlighted in the use of a perspective depends not only on the perspective used—person-focused perspective, theme-focused perspective, or context-focused perspective—but on the personal perspective to which the three perspectives are applied. We can apply the perspectives either to the Father's knowledge of the Son,

5   Poythress, *Knowing and the Trinity*, 83–89.

or to the Son's knowledge of the Father, or to the Spirit's knowledge of the depths of God.

We have chosen to focus on these three forms of personal knowledge, because the Bible explicitly mentions them. But, because of the indwelling of persons in the Trinity, we may reasonably infer that within the Trinity each person knows each other person. And that knowledge takes place in the context of the third person. So, for example, the Spirit knows the Father in the context of the Son.

Each of the three personal perspectives has a close relation to analogy. This conclusion follows because of the close relation between perspectives and analogies. Perspectives use analogies because they invoke background knowledge in the course of taking a view of the object. The background knowledge is brought into relation to the object. So, for example, if Alice uses a perspective of health in viewing her pet rabbit, the health of the rabbit is brought into relation to what Alice already knows about health from her experiences or reading. So one way of expressing the use of analogy is to say that there is an analogy between things in the context on the one hand, and the object that is the focus of knowledge on the other hand.

Conversely, analogies always involve the use of a perspective. How so? Analogies are always analogies used by someone. That someone, by using an analogy, is also developing a perspective on the knowledge that is offered through the analogy. Our human reasoning uses both analogies and perspectives. In both ways, we are dependent on ways in which God has organized the world and organized our knowledge. It is God who is the ultimate source, whose patterns are reflected in human reasoning.

We can see the presence of analogy more aptly if, instead of focusing on divine knowledge, we look at an instance of ectypal knowledge, knowledge by human beings. To this we turn in the next chapter.

17

Perspectives on Our Knowledge of God

LET US CONSIDER our human knowledge of God. Each of us is personally involved in what he or she knows. Any one person's knowledge of God has the form of a personal perspective on God. This personal perspective is mentioned in the last part of Matthew 11:27:

> All things have been handed over to me by my Father, and no one knows the Son except the Father, and no one knows the Father except the Son and *anyone to whom the Son chooses to reveal him.*

The text speaks about "anyone to whom the Son chooses to reveal him." One such person is the apostle Peter. Through the revelation given by the Son, the apostle Peter comes to have personal knowledge of the Father. This personal knowledge is an expression of the personal perspective of Peter. Here is an instance of a personal perspective by a human being.

Personal Perspective from Matthew 11:27

In the previous chapter we looked at the knowledge within the Trinity. We especially focused on the Father's knowledge of the Son and the Son's knowledge of the Father. We also acknowledged that the Holy Spirit has a role in the personal knowledge in the Trinity. In addition to all of this, knowledge belongs also to "anyone to whom the Son chooses to reveal him [the Father]" (Matt. 11:27).

With this knowledge as our object of study, we now apply the three perspectives on a perspective. First, the person-focused perspective focuses on the person who knows (such as Peter). The person is "anyone." It is any human being to whom the Son reveals the Father.

Second, the theme-focused perspective focuses on the theme by which knowledge is received. It is human knowledge of God. And in the final part of Matthew 11:27, the central focus for the object of knowledge is the Father. The Father is the theme of the knowledge. In knowing the Father, we know God. But the focus on the Father as a distinct person functions like a theme, focusing our attention.

Third, the context-focused perspective focuses on the context in which the knowledge arises and is provided. The context is preeminently in the Son. Because the Son knows the Father, as affirmed earlier in verse 27, he is in a position to reveal such knowledge to a human being.

As usual, knowledge involves an analogy between the theme on the one hand and the context on the other. We see the Father through the Son. So we use as a context or as a background for knowing the Father what we have come to know with respect to the Son. The analogy holds, because the Son is "the exact imprint of his nature" (Heb. 1:3). (See table 17.1.)

Table 17.1: Perspectives on Human Knowledge of God

human knower	The Father as representative of God	The Son as revealer
person-focused perspective	theme-focused perspective	context-focused perspective

Matthew 11:27 does not explicitly mention the role of the Holy Spirit. But we know from other passages, such as 1 Corinthians 2:10–16, that the Holy Spirit enables people to understand the Christian message. The Spirit is the Spirit of Christ (Rom. 8:9–11). He shows us the things of Christ (Eph. 1:17–19; 1 John 2:20–27).

Confirmation of the Son's Mediatorial Role

Other passages confirm the central role that the Son has in giving the knowledge of God:

> Jesus said to him, "I am the way, and the truth, and the life. No one comes to the Father except through me." (John 14:6)

> Whoever has seen me has seen the Father. (John 14:9)

> And this is eternal life, that they know you, the only true God, and Jesus Christ whom you have sent. . . .
>
> I have manifested your name to the people whom you gave me out of the world. Yours they were, and you gave them to me, and they have kept your word. Now they know that everything that you have given me is from you. For I have given them the words that you gave me, and they have received them and have come to know in truth that I came from you; and they have believed that you sent me. (John 17:3, 6–8)

Human Knowledge of God as Perspectival

In sum, we have three aspects in our knowledge of God. The aspect in focus in the person-focused perspective is the person who knows—the person to whom the Son reveals knowledge. The aspect in focus in the theme-focused perspective is the Father. The aspect in focus in the context-focused perspective is the Son, through whom we know the Father.

So we can say that human knowledge of God has a perspectival structure. This perspectival structure reflects and imitates the structure with respect to the Father's knowledge of the Son and the Son's knowledge of the Father. This structural imitation is hinted at in Matthew 11:27, where Jesus puts side by side his knowledge of the Father and our human knowledge of the Father: "no one knows the Father except the Son *and* anyone to whom the Son chooses to reveal him."

Human reasoning as one aspect in human knowledge takes place within this environment in which the pattern of God's personal knowledge is reflected in human beings.

The human knowledge of God involves perspective and analogy. Human perspective imitates and reflects divine perspective. The fundamental analogy is the analogy between the Son who reveals and the Father who is revealed. This analogy exists in God even before the Father sends the Son to earth to accomplish the divine revelation.

18

Perspectives on Analogies in General

TO CONFIRM FURTHER how human reasoning reflects the Trinity, we can also apply the triad of perspectives on a perspective to the general case of analogy.

A Lodge in a Cucumber Field

It is convenient to consider a particular case. Let us remember Isaiah 1:8. It says that "the daughter of Zion is left . . . like a lodge in a cucumber field." Here we have an analogy between the daughter of Zion and a lodge in a cucumber field. The cucumber field is what Max Black calls the "subsidiary subject," in terms of which the author says something about the principal subject, which is the daughter of Zion. The lodge serves as a *perspective* on the daughter of Zion.

Let us analyze this analogy using the three perspectives on a perspective. First, the person-focused perspective focuses on the person who pays attention to the analogy. (Of course, the writer, both divine and human, also has a perspective. But it is convenient to focus on what happens as the reader attempts to understand.) The analogy is not effective in communication unless there is a person who can potentially grasp it. The person in question is any reader or hearer of the book of Isaiah. The person endeavors to figure out what are the significant points of comparison between the daughter of Zion and the lodge in a cucumber field.

Second, the theme-focused perspective focuses on the theme in the passage, namely the daughter of Zion, which is the principal subject for the metaphor.

Third, the context-focused perspective focuses on the context in which the person's knowledge grows. The key context is the subsidiary subject, which is the lodge in a cucumber field. The subsidiary subject is supposed to be a source of background knowledge to the person, in order to inform him about the state of the daughter of Zion. (See table 18.1.)

Table 18.1: Perspectives on Isaiah 1:8

theme-focused perspective	context-focused perspective	person-focused perspective
the daughter of Zion	a lodge in a cucumber field	person using the analogy

The Interaction of Principal Subject and Subsidiary Subject

As we indicated earlier in our discussion of metaphor, metaphors operate by the interaction of a principal subject and a subsidiary subject (ch. 9). Understanding a metaphor involves a kind of implicit reasoning. So it is a further instance of reasoning in which we may see reflections of patterns from the Trinity.

The instance with a lodge in a cucumber field illustrates a general pattern, namely that metaphors in general can be analyzed using the triad of perspectives on a perspective. The person contemplating the metaphor corresponds to the person-focused perspective. The principal subject of the metaphor corresponds to the theme-focused perspective. The subsidiary subject of the metaphor corresponds to the context-focused perspective. This correspondence works because any metaphor functions like a perspective. The subsidiary subject is used as a window or perspective on the principal subject, in order to reveal something about the principal subject.

These observations confirm for us the perspectival character of knowledge supplied by metaphors. The three perspectives on a perspective coinhere, reflecting the coinherence of the persons of the Trinity. One implication is that metaphors are irreducibly mysterious.

PART VI

SIMPLICITY AND THE DOCTRINE OF GOD

We explore the relation of simplicity to perspectives and analogies used in knowing God.

19

The Simplicity of God
and Perspectives

WE MAY NOW CONSIDER how the doctrine of the simplicity of God is relevant to our thinking about perspectives and analogies as forms of reasoning. What does it mean for God to be "simple"? And what implications does this have for our thinking about perspectives and analogies and the way we reason?

The Idea of Simplicity

The word *simple*, when applied to God, has a special meaning. To be "simple" means not to be divisible into parts.[1] God cannot be divided up. In particular, the three persons of the Trinity are not three "parts" of God. One person is not one third of God. Rather, each person is fully God. All the attributes of God, such as his unchangeability and his omniscience, belong to God as a whole, and they belong to each person of the Trinity. The attributes cannot be split up, any more than God can be split up into parts.

One aspect of simplicity is that any one attribute, such as omniscience or omnipotence or eternality, belongs to the whole of God.

---

1 Vern S. Poythress, *The Mystery of the Trinity: A Trinitarian Approach to the Attributes of God* (Phillipsburg, NJ: P&R, 2020), chs. 9 and 43; Francis Turretin, *Institutes of Elenctic Theology*, 3 vols. (Phillipsburg, NJ: P&R, 1992), 1.191 (III.vii.3).

God's omnipotence is an omniscient and eternal omnipotence. Each attribute functions like a perspective on everything that God is, rather than being a description of only one "piece" (as if there were pieces).

Implications for Human Knowledge

Our human knowledge of God is limited, because we are finite. But it can still be true. And our human knowledge reflects God's knowledge of himself, though the reflection is a derivative reflection and we remain finite while God remains infinite. We can see that, in our own thinking about God's attributes, each attribute functions as a perspective. This perspectival character of the attributes is an implication of God's being simple.

Now, God is the ultimate source for all perspectives and for all analogies. He is the archetype. Each person of the Trinity has a personal perspective associated with his divine knowledge. Each person is "analogous" to the other persons. And this form of analogy is the archetypal form of analogy.

The simplicity has effects when reflected in the world. Human knowledge, and the structure of the world itself, is filled with perspectives and analogies. The perspectives can be expected to function as perspectives on the whole of truth. Truth originates in God, and any truth that we have comes as a gift from God (Ps. 94:10b), reflecting God's own infinite knowledge of the truth.

In God the truth is simple, because God is simple, just as God is omnipotent and God is eternal. The three personal perspectives within the Trinity, one for each person of the Trinity, are perspectives on the whole truth, which is unified.

Perspectives on the Whole

By analogy, within human experience, perspectives can be expected to be perspectives on the whole. Analogies used within perspectives will be analogies that can be used with respect to the whole field of knowledge. (See fig. 19.1.)

Figure 19.1: Perspectives in God and in Human Knowledge

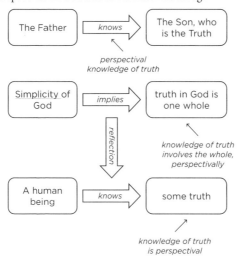

As mentioned in chapter 6, C. S. Lewis sees the pervasiveness of analogy in human knowledge: "we have seen since [in the course of the arguments developed in Lewis's article] that all our truth, or all but a few fragments, is won by metaphor."[2] He allows that there could be an exception, when he says, "all but a few fragments." In the context in which he writes, it appears that he is allowing for an exception when knowledge comes by direct sensation. For example, we do not need a metaphor to see an area of red color in front of us. And when we see it, we know something: we know that there is red in front of us. But we do need to understand that it is red, rather than some other color. And that is an instance of classification, which involves analogy (ch. 6). One instance of red is analogous to other instances of the same color.

The use of an analogy with other instances of red is only the beginning of our use of analogy. There is a wider analogy with other instances within the wider category of color sensations. And then there is a still wider analogy with other instances within the category of sensations

---

2   C. S. Lewis, "Bluspels and Flalansferes: A Semantic Nightmare," in *Selected Literary Essays*, 251–65 [265], ed. Walter Hooper (Cambridge: Cambridge University Press, 1969).

of all kinds (hearing and feeling as well as seeing). In addition, there is the wider category of experiences (of which sensation is only one aspect, simultaneous with many others). Experiences of conversations are not reducible to sensations. Rather, we experience verbal meanings, not just audible sounds. So the experience of red becomes a window or a perspective on human experience in general. (See fig. 19.2.)

Figure 19.2: An Instance of Red, within the Larger Field of Personal Experience

In addition, any bit of human experience has analogies with other human experiences. And these all have their ultimate root or archetype in divine activity. (See fig. 19.3.)

Figure 19.3: Personal Experiences as Analogous

God is the original one who knows and loves. Knowing and loving are activities of God, the one God, and they are also activities between any two of the persons of the Trinity.[3] So we end with a pervasive presence of analogies, rooted in the ultimate mystery of the relations between persons in the Trinity.

If analogies are pervasive, by the same token perspectives are pervasive, because analogies are closely related to perspectives. The ar-

---

3   Poythress, *Mystery of the Trinity*, chs. 44 and 47.

chetypal perspectives are the three personal perspectives of the three persons of the Trinity. Human beings imitate the Trinity when they consider analogies, because the use of an analogy involves a perspective by the person who is using the analogy.

20

Using Analogies in
the Doctrine of God

THE SIMPLICITY OF GOD also encourages us to explore how we as human beings discuss the doctrine of God. How do we go about describing God?

If all of our thought and reasoning is analogical, our thinking and reasoning about God is also analogical.

Anthropomorphic Language

The presence of analogy is more obvious in the case of *anthropomorphic* language about God. Anthropomorphic language is language describing God by analogy with human beings.[1] In the Bible, God says that he speaks and plans and loves. By using such language, God indicates that his activities are analogous to the activities of human beings who speak and plan and love. As usual, these analogies are not identities. God is the Creator, while human beings are creatures. We use such analogies in speaking about God because God himself uses them. They have meaning.

Technical Terms for God

It might seem that we can escape the use of analogy by employing technical terms like *infinity* or *omniscience* to describe God. But in the

---

1   Vern S. Poythress, *The Mystery of the Trinity: A Trinitarian Approach to the Attributes of God* (Phillipsburg, NJ: P&R, 2020), ch. 14; Wayne A. Grudem, *Systematic Theology*, 2nd ed. (Grand Rapids, MI: Zondervan, 2020), 188–89.

background we still rely on analogies in establishing special meanings for technical terms. We also use analogies in explaining to other people what the terms mean.[2]

Moreover, the doctrine of the simplicity of God implies that we cannot effectively isolate the distinct terms from one another, nor can we isolate the distinct affirmations that we make about God using anthropomorphic language. All the affirmations function more like perspectives on the whole of God than like descriptions of some one feature of God, a feature that we could claim to be isolated from everything else about God. (See fig. 20.1.)

Figure 20.1: Affirmations about God as Not Isolated

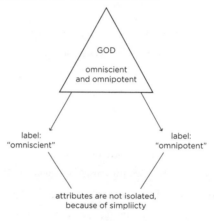

Limitations in Classical Division of Topics

The principle of analogy applies also when we are reasoning about God. We use analogies. Consider the common ways of organizing the discussion about God into distinct topics. Often discussion starts with truths about the unity of God, including the attributes of God. Then, as a separate section, there follows a discussion of the Trinity. Then there

---

2   Poythress, *Mystery of the Trinity*, chs. 17 and 19; C. S. Lewis, "Bluspels and Flalansferes: A Semantic Nightmare," in *Selected Literary Essays*, 251–65, ed. Walter Hooper (Cambridge: Cambridge University Press, 1969); C. S. Lewis, *Letters to Malcolm: Chiefly on Prayer* (New York: Harcourt, Brace & World, 1964), 51–52.

may be a discussion of God's actions with respect to the world. The discussion may proceed from the eternal plan of God to activities in creating the world and governing it (providence; miracle). We reason from one topic to another.

Some kind of division in topics makes sense, because in a topical arrangement it is impossible to discuss all the topics at once. Yet the topics cannot be isolated from each other.

The simplicity of God is usually discussed as one of the attributes of God, within the larger topic of the unity of the one God. Simplicity is sometimes treated as a kind of "master" attribute, because it is used to specify the relation of the attributes to each other and to God himself.

Might we also treat simplicity as a perspective on God? If so, by the logic of simplicity itself, it is a perspective not only on the unity of God, but on each of the persons of the Trinity. Augustine does something similar to this move when he argues for the deity of the Son and the deity of the Holy Spirit by appealing to simplicity. The basic argument runs that, if the Son has a divine attribute, such as being eternal or simply being divine, he must have all the attributes of God. That is because the attributes cannot be separated (according to the principle of God being simple). Accordingly, the Son is fully God. The same argument holds for the Holy Spirit.[3] These are reasonings that depend on analogies.

The doctrine of the Trinity can be explained using two key terms: *essence* and *person*. In God there is one essence and three persons. So the word *essence* functions to designate what belongs to the oneness of God. The word *person* functions to designate what belongs to the multiplicity or threeness in God. That is appropriate. Both words have mystery in them. They do not actually *separate* between the oneness and the threeness. That is impossible, because God is inseparable, as the principle of simplicity affirms.

---

3 Augustine, *On the Trinity*, in *A Select Library of the Nicene and Post-Nicene Fathers of the Christian Church*, vol. 3, ed. Philip Schaff (Grand Rapids, MI: Eerdmans, 1978), 100 (book 6, ch. 4, §6; and book 6, ch. 5, §7); Poythress, *Mystery of the Trinity*, ch. 26.

But if the aspects of the two topics are inseparable, how do we in fact construe them?

In fact, the essence does not exist except with the persons; the persons do not exist except with the essence.

In expounding either topic, we actually presuppose the reality of the truths belonging to the complementary topic. Each attribute of God, and also the entire essence of God, is there in each person. Conversely, each person has each attribute. Reasoning takes place within this larger environment. We know other truths, which help us to understand any one truth.

21

Conclusion

WHAT IS OUR CONCLUSION? We may summarize in a few short statements.

All human knowledge is analogical. Our thinking imitates and reflects God's thoughts. But this basic analogy is also reflected in the work of analogies within human thought. We see things from somewhere. There are analogies between our background knowledge and our current focus.

These analogies have their origin in the perfect knowledge of God. This knowledge is one and three, because God is one God and three persons. The similarities and distinctions between persons are the foundation for similarities and distinctions that exist in analogies.

Human knowledge cannot ascend into an ideal realm with a direct divine vision, which dispenses with analogy.

Human reasoning is analogical reasoning.

Human knowledge of God is the indispensable background for our knowledge of anything at all (Ps. 94:10; Job 32:8).

These realities should encourage us to be humble and to be in awe of God. At the same time, we should rejoice in the genuine knowledge of God that he gives us through Christ the Son (Matt. 11:27).

APPENDIXES ON MODELING ANALOGIES

*We offer some articles dealing in a more technical
way with the use of contrast, variation, and
distribution, and their relation to analogy.*

Modeling the Complexity of Analogy

REASONING WITH ANALOGY may seem less tractable and less satisfying than syllogistic reasoning or other forms of deduction within formal logic. Analogies are not fully formalized. And it seems that there are innate limitations to formalization, so that analogical reasoning can never be fully captured in a formalized system.[1]

The lack of neat, clean models can be partially remedied. There is a way to offer a quasi-mathematical model for analogical reasoning. But the model has to be more complex than what is customary for syllogisms and for other kinds of formal logic.

The full discussion of this kind of model belongs to more technical literature.[2] But in this and the subsequent appendix, we can offer some context for understanding how it is possible to represent analogy.

Three Aspects of Analogy

We may begin by returning to the observations made earlier about the nature of analogy (chs. 4–5, esp. table 4.2 and fig. 4.7). Analogy involves

---

[1] Vern S. Poythress, *Logic: A God-Centered Approach to the Foundation of Western Thought* (Wheaton, IL: Crossway, 2013), ch. 17; Vern S. Poythress, "Semiotic Analysis of Symbolic Logic Using Tagmemic Theory: With Implications for Analytic Philosophy," *Semiotica* 2021, https://doi.org/10.1515/sem-2020-0018, https://frame-poythress.org/a-semiotic-analysis-of-symbolic-logic-using-tagmemic-theory-with-implications-for-analytic-philosophy/.

[2] Vern S. Poythress, "Information-Theoretic Confirmation of Semiotic Structures," *Semiotica* 193 (2013): 67–82.

similarities, differences, and the analogical relation itself. This threefold character belonging to analogy has an affinity to a triad of perspectives in the study of language: contrast, variation, and distribution (ch. 4).

In the case of both triads, each perspective interlocks with the others. All three occur together. The interlocking is what makes representation in a model more challenging. We achieve an "easier" representation in the case of a syllogistic pattern because contrast is further heightened and variation and distribution are displaced to the background. This alteration takes place by artificial isolation of the meanings within a syllogism from the complexity of meanings in the full system of ordinary language.

So how do we represent the interlocking of contrast, variation, and distribution in ordinary language? Or, alternatively, how do we represent similarities, differences, and an analogical relation?

The Use of Probability

We can begin to represent some complexities if we bring in the use of probability. Consider the case with syllogisms. Syllogisms are supposed to work 100 percent of the time. But in the complexities of life, we have to deal with less than complete certainties. If we consider 100 syllogisms that are being applied to ordinary life, we may find that a small percentage of them involve an equivocation in meaning. For example, consider an example that has actually been used to illustrate how syllogisms work:

All men are mortal.
Socrates is a man.
Therefore, Socrates is mortal.

The reasoning may seem to be straightforward. But does it apply now that Socrates is dead? When Socrates was alive within this world, it would have seemed natural to apply the syllogism in a context where the word *mortal* means being subject to future physical death. But the Bible teaches that people continue to exist after bodily death. So, after

Socrates's body has been laid to rest, "mortal" might then still mean "subject to future physical death," or it might mean having already suffered the penalty of physical death. Or it might mean an annihilation of the person himself (which the Bible does not teach). The ambiguities mean that the syllogism may or may not work, depending on which meaning or meanings we have in mind for the word *mortal.*

We can then examine a large number of syllogisms in such contexts. Based on our sample, we might say that syllogistic reasoning is valid 98 percent of the time. There is a 98 percent probability, a probability of 0.98, that a syllogism chosen at random from our sample will be an instance of valid reasoning.

In many situations, the probabilities that we predict for various events in language depend on previous knowledge. And that previous knowledge is changing over time. The probabilities may also vary from person to person, because different people may have different amounts of access to various pieces of information. The introduction of probabilities, and the representation of uncertainty, brings complexity. And the introduction of a variety of persons introduces complexity. But complexity is needed in a model to represent some forms of complexity in the world.

Questions about Language

We can now consider a large number of different types of questions that we could ask about occurrences of events involving language. For simplicity, we can imagine that each question must be a yes-no question. And we attach to each question a corresponding probability, from the analyst's point of view. What does the analyst think is the probability that person A will utter the word "go" at a certain time T?

Within this context of using probabilities, how do we represent the triad of contrast, variation, and distribution? We might say that we are looking for a probabilistic "model."

Within a probabilistic representation or model, the idea of *contrast* in language corresponds to the claim that two questions do not simultaneously have a "yes" answer. If the word "go" is being uttered, then we will not simultaneously see the word "come" uttered by the same person at the same time. That means that the probability of getting a "yes" answer to both questions is 0 or nearly 0. In the notation of probability, P("go", by person A at time T; & "come" by person A at time T) ~ 0. ("~" symbolizes "is approximately equal to".)

Now consider the idea of *variation*. Variation means variation in distinct occurrences of instances of the same larger category. So, for example, one person says "go" in a loud voice, and another in a soft voice. But both occurrences are occurrences of the word "go." The idea of variation in language corresponds within a probabilistic model to the claim that a "yes" answer to one question implies a "yes" answer to a second question. If "go" is uttered in a loud voice, it always implies that "go" is uttered.

Third, we consider *distribution*. Distribution is the framework or environment in which a particular language unit is expected to occur. But units are typically semi-independent of their environments, in order to be recognizable as units at all. This semi-independence corresponds to the concept of probabilistic independence, or at least approximate independence.

This independence can be illustrated by any number of examples. Consider the utterance "This dog is brown." The unit "dog" is semi-independent of the contextual frame, which consists in the surrounding material plus a blank: "This _____ is brown." This frame remains the same, whatever noun is put into the blank. And whatever noun is put into the blank can be put into many other frames, such as "The boy fed the ____." So the frame and what fills the frame (in this case a noun) are semi-independent. In general, within the theory of probability, two events A and B are probabilistically independent when $P(A) \times P(B) = P(A \ \& \ B)$. This condition for independence is equivalent to saying $P(A \mid B) = P(A)$, where $P(A \mid B)$ denotes the "conditional" probability of A, given that we know that B occurs. The condition $P(A \mid B) = P(A)$ means that the knowledge that B occurs does not influence the probability of A, which is intuitively what we mean by "independence."

As a result, contrast, variation, and distribution all are represented together, and interlocked with each other, in a probabilistic model.

Once we have such a probabilistic model, we can apply it to instances of analogy. Analogy, we have said, involves similarities, differences, and the relation of analogy itself. The similarities represent a contrast between the two similar things on the one hand, and the rest of the world on the other hand. The differences are variations in a general pattern. And the analogy itself corresponds to distribution. The two things that are analogous can nevertheless be considered distinctly. Typically, they belong to two distinct arenas of information. There is a principal subject, which is in focus. And there is a subsidiary subject, through which we say something about the principal subject, by invoking an analogy between the two subjects. The two subjects are approximately independent.

We describe an analogy using the term *similarities* in the plural, and the term *differences* in the plural. Typically we have to deal with a whole collection or suite of similarities, which are clustered together in the operation of the analogy. So we have not one but a suite of elements that contrast with what is unlike them. Each element is represented by its own probability condition, namely a condition of mutual exclusion. Likewise, when we have a whole suite of differences, each difference is represented by its own probability condition, which consists in an implication.

The result is that the overall model becomes complicated. It is many-dimensional. Many kinds of yes-no questions may make up the whole. Though there is complexity, there is also coherence. There is nothing scatterbrained about it. Such a model may therefore help people who feel that the idea of analogical reasoning is too vague and too uncontrollable. Analogy is *not* a matter of pure subjectivity. We do not invite ourselves to jump to a merely arbitrary result, without guidelines for the jump. Rather, there is underlying rationality. It is a more complex rationality than in the case of the artificially crafted, isolated environment in which a syllogism functions well because we have carefully crafted the environment to guarantee univocal meaning.

In the next appendix we provide references to other illustrations concerning the use of contrast, variation, and distribution.

Analysis Using Analogy

WE NOW DRAW ATTENTION to a number of published articles that use analogy in a tightly controlled way. These articles illustrate that analogy is widespread, and that the use of analogy is one reasonable path in analyzing human meanings. These uses harmonize with the role of analogy in appendix A.

We would have liked to include these articles in full, as appendices. But the copyright restrictions on them has not made that feasible. Fortunately, the full text of the articles is available on the internet. We have provided links for accessing them:

Vern S. Poythress, "A Simple Traffic-Light Semiotic Model for Tagmemic Theory," *Semiotica* 2018:225 (November 2018): 253–67, https://doi .org/10.1515/sem-2017-0025. Available for download at https://frame -poythress.org/a-simple-traffic-light-semiotic-model-for-tagmemic -theory/.

Vern S. Poythress, "Semiotic Analysis of Symbolic Logic Using Tagmemic Theory: With Implications for Analytic Philosophy," *Semiotica* 2021, https://doi.org/10.1515/sem-2020-0018. Available for download at https://frame-poythress.org/semiotic-analysis-of -symbolic-logic-using-tagmemic-theory-with-implications-for -analytic-philosophy/.

Vern S. Poythress, "A Semiotic Analysis of Multiple Systems of Logic: Using Tagmemic Theory to Assess the Usefulness and Limitations of Formal Logics, and to Produce a Mathematical Lattice Model Including Multiple Systems of Logic," *Semiotica* 2021, doi.org/10.1515/sem-2020-0051. Available for download at https://frame-poythress.org/a-semiotic-analysis-of-multiple-systems-of-logic-using-tagmemic-theory-to-assess-the-usefulness-and-limitations-of-formal-logics-and-to-produce-a-mathematical-lattice-model-including-multiple-systems-of-logic/.

Bibliography

The Athanasian Creed. https://www.ccel.org/creeds/athanasian.creed.html (accessed April 4, 2020).

Augustine. *On the Trinity.* In *A Select Library of the Nicene and Post-Nicene Fathers of the Christian Church*, volume 3. Edited by Philip Schaff. Grand Rapids, MI: Eerdmans, 1978.

Black, Max. *Models and Metaphors: Studies in Language and Philosophy.* Ithaca, NY: Cornell University Press, 1962.

Encyclopedia Britannica. "Laws of thought: Logic," https://www.britannica.com/topic/laws-of-thought, accessed April 14, 2020.

Frame, John M. *The Doctrine of the Knowledge of God.* Phillipsburg, NJ: P&R, 1987.

Frame, John M. *Perspectives on the Word of God: An Introduction to Christian Ethics.* Eugene, OR: Wipf & Stock, 1999.

Frame, John M. "A Primer on Perspectivalism (Revised 2008)," https://frame-poythress.org/a-primer-on-perspectivalism-revised-2008/, accessed April 25, 2020.

Gregory of Nazianzus, "Oration 40: The Oration on Holy Baptism," https://www.newadvent.org/fathers/310240.htm, accessed May 16, 2020.

Kuhn, Thomas S. *The Structure of Scientific Revolutions.* Chicago: University of Chicago Press, 1970.

Letham, Robert. *The Holy Trinity: In Scripture, History, Theology, and Worship.* Revised and expanded. Phillipsburg, NJ: P&R, 2019.

Lewis, C. S. "Bluspels and Flalansferes: A Semantic Nightmare." In *Selected Literary Essays*, 251–65. Edited by Walter Hooper. Cambridge: Cambridge University Press, 1969.

Lewis, C. S. *Letters to Malcolm: Chiefly on Prayer*. New York: Harcourt, Brace & World, 1964.

Merriam-Webster online dictionary, https://www.merriam-webster.com /dictionary/analogy, accessed April 11, 2020.

Nicene-Constantinopolitan Creed, https://orthodoxwiki.org/Nicene -Constantinopolitan_Creed, accessed April 11, 2020.

Owen, John. *A Brief Declaration and Vindication of the Doctrine of the Trinity*. 1669. In *The Works of John Owen*. 16 vols. Edited by William H. Goold, 2:365–454. Reprint, Edinburgh/Carlisle, PA: The Banner of Truth Trust, 1965.

Owen, John. *Communion with the Triune God*. Edited by Kelly M. Kapic and Justin Taylor. Wheaton, IL: Crossway, 2007.

Polanyi, Michael. *Personal Knowledge: Towards a Post-Critical Philosophy*. Chicago: University of Chicago Press, 1964.

Polanyi, Michael. *The Tacit Dimension*. Garden City, NY: Anchor Books, 1967.

Poythress, Vern S. "Information-Theoretic Confirmation of Semiotic Structures," *Semiotica* 193 (2013): 67–82. DOI 10.1515/sem-2013-0004.

Poythress, Vern S. *Knowing and the Trinity: How Perspectives in Human Knowledge Imitate the Trinity*. Phillipsburg, NJ: P&R, 2018.

Poythress, Vern S. *Logic: A God-Centered Approach to the Foundation of Western Thought*. Wheaton, IL: Crossway, 2013.

Poythress, Vern S. *The Lordship of Christ: Serving Our Savior All of the Time, in All of Life, with All of Our Heart*. Wheaton, IL: Crossway, 2016.

Poythress, Vern S. *The Mystery of the Trinity: A Trinitarian Approach to the Attributes of God*. Phillipsburg, NJ: P&R, 2020.

Poythress, Vern S. *Redeeming Science: A God-Centered Approach*. Wheaton, IL: Crossway, 2006.

Poythress, Vern S. "Reforming Ontology and Logic in the Light of the Trinity: An Application of Van Til's Idea of Analogy," *Westminster Theological Journal* 57 (1995): 187–219.

Poythress, Vern S. "A Semiotic Analysis of Multiple Systems of Logic: Using Tagmemic Theory to Assess the Usefulness and Limitations of Formal Logics, and to Produce a Mathematical Lattice Model Including Multiple

Systems of Logic," *Semiotica* 2021 (January 2022), doi.org/10.1515/sem-2020-0051, https://frame-poythress.org/a-semiotic-analysis-of-multiple-systems-of-logic-using-tagmemic-theory-to-assess-the-usefulness-and-limitations-of-formal-logics-and-to-produce-a-mathematical-lattice-model-including-multiple-systems-of-logic/.

Poythress, Vern S. "Semiotic Analysis of Symbolic Logic Using Tagmemic Theory: With Implications for Analytic Philosophy," *Semiotica* 2021, https://doi.org/10.1515/sem-2020-0018, https://frame-poythress.org/a-semiotic-analysis-of-symbolic-logic-using-tagmemic-theory-with-implications-for-analytic-philosophy/.

Poythress, Vern S. "A Simple Traffic-Light Semiotic Model for Tagmemic Theory," *Semiotica* 2018:225 (November 2018): 253–67, https://doi.org/10.1515/sem-2017-0025. https://frame-poythress.org/a-simple-traffic-light-semiotic-model-for-tagmemic-theory/.

Poythress, Vern S. *Symphonic Theology: The Validity of Multiple Perspectives in Theology.* Reprint. Phillipsburg, NJ: P&R, 2001.

Ross, J. F. *Portraying Analogy.* Cambridge: Cambridge University Press, 1981.

Toulmin, Stephen Edelston. *The Uses of Argument.* Cambridge: Cambridge University Press, 1958.

Turretin, Francis. *Institutes of Elenctic Theology.* Translated by George Musgrave Giger. Edited by James T. Dennison Jr. 3 vols. Phillipsburg, NJ: P&R, 1992.

Wittgenstein, Ludwig. *Tractatus Logico-Philosophicus: The German Text of Logisch-philosophische Abhandlung.* Translated by D. F. Pears & B. F. McGuinness, with introduction by Bertrand Russell. London: Routledge & Kegan Paul/New York: Humanities Press, 1963.

General Index

Scripture Index

Also Available from
Vern S. Poythress

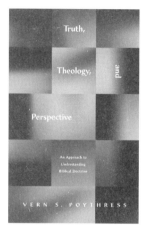

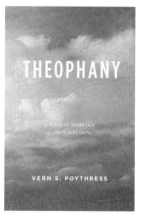

For more information, visit **crossway.org**.